Maybe it's just me...

more titles by Barry Parham

Why I Hate Straws

An offbeat worldview of an offbeat world

Sorry, We Can't Use Funny

Blush

Politics and other unnatural acts

The Middle-Age of Aquarius

Full Frontal Stupidity

Chariots of Ire

You Gonna Finish That Dragon?

Maybe

it's just me...

Barry Parham

ISBN: 15118-13091
ISBN-13: 978-15-1181-3099

Contents

Dedication

This humor collection is dedicated to Robin Williams.

Thanks for it all, man.

Introduction

Welcome back!

This new collection contains humor columns written between July 2013 and May 2014, an overly odd time by *anybody's* standards.

Russia hosted the Winter Olympics...at a Black Sea beach resort. It ended up being the most expensive Winter Games in history, despite the Kremlin's attempts to pull off the entire opening ceremonies with only two AAA batteries.

The world said 'goodbye' to Nelson Mandela in a televised event translated by the world's most incompetent interpreter, if you don't count Toronto Mayor Rob Ford.

Notorious Boston gangster Whitey Bulger was convicted and got two life sentences, plus five more years. (The five extra years was a desperate attempt by Bostonians to thwart the threat of a Ben Affleck movie about Whitey Bulger.)

Barack Obama was sworn in for the second time, although he was sworn AT way more times.

Army private Bradley Manning leaked 700,000 sensitive files and then changed his name to Chelsea, which stumped Homeland Security for over 18 months.

In Malaysia, an entire plane vanished, prompting conspiracy theorists to suggest the plane had changed its name to Chelsea.

And in a secret midnight vote, Congress voted to not raise taxes.

I made that last part up.

Really.

Hey, It's Not Rocket Surgery

now trending online: morons

<>~<>~~~~~~~~~~<>~<>~~~~~~~~~~<>~<>

Let's play a game. Here's how it works: I'll show you something somebody said on facebook, and you try to guess if that person has a cerebral cortex.

Sounds simple, right? Based solely on someone's facebook posts, you can determine if they're a functional, contributing member of society, of if they spent their formative years running into trees, missing doorways, and eating lead paint.

We'll start with an easy one:

Its mind bottling how dumb she is.

Yeah, it bottles the mind, all right. Somebody contact the school district: we definitely want to hold this little bundle of joy back a grate. It's Ann & Nigma, is what it is.

Here's another:

That was no reason for her to delittle me.

Oh, I'm guessing there's an absolute *raft* of reasons for her to "delittle" you. But you shouldn't be butter about it.

And again:

Every post I read this pass week was full of misteaks.

Whew. Irony you could land a plane on. (...or, in the case of Malaysian Airlines, hide a plane under.)

And it's not just facebook *users* making mistake mistakes. The so-called facebook professionals have fat fingers, too. For example...you know those irritating quizzes that have started popping up on facebook about forty times a day? Those alleged personality-mining probes that address burning topics like these?

- Which One Of Snow White's Dwarfs Are You?
- Which Star Wars Droid In A Crowd Scene With No Speaking Lines Would You Be?
- What Kind Of Incurable Intestinal Disorder Are You?

Yeah, those. Well, check out this one's title:

What Were You In A Past Live?

Hmm. I don't know what you were in a "past live," Mr. Mint-Condition Brain Pan, but my five bucks says you weren't a returning *Jeopardy* champion.

For our honeymoon, were stayin at the Embassy Sweets.

Mmm hmm. Too bad you're not honeymooning in France. You could stay at the Paris Hilton.

The weirdest part is that every toy in today's gadget arsenal not only comes with spell-check built in; it comes with spell-check *enabled*. You practically have to call tech support and attend a three-day seminar to figure out how to turn spell-check *off*.

By then it was a mute point.

Your co-workers wish *you* were a mute point.

In our mad stampede to embrace social media during the last two generations, we've trampled a number of innocents along the way: spelling; handwriting; the petty limitations of having just two genders. Punctuation takes way too long, and capital letters have become as rare as beef at Taco Bell.

my fav was the winner whoot!

(Editor's note: I would like to make the comment that "woot" was misspelled in the previous sentence, but I'm afraid of being flattened by a giant sarcasm meteor.)

I'm sick of are society as a hole.

First of all, it's not yore society, dude. Back of.

Dude u have 2 take what she says with a grade of slaw.

Dude. You are the slaw of the earth.

But facebook's just one factor of social media. Let's turn now to the Text Messengers: the barely recognizable humanoid aliens from Planet Smart Phone. These are bizarre life forms who apparently draw energy from small handheld devices that cost more than your first car. The aliens spend their lives speed-typing misspelled words with their thumbs until they grow hunchbacked and walk smack into fountains at the mall.

But they're infiltrating our culture. Nowadays, when you go to see a play or to hear the symphony, there's a new preliminary element to the event. Before the curtain rises or the baton snaps, an announcer has to make a formal request *asking the audience not to text during the show.*

Here's an average "conversation" you might see on a smart phone between two aliens named, say, Biffy and Muffy:

Biffy: so i said r u going 2 the mal
Muffy: lol
Biffy: mall
Muffy: rotfl
Biffy: he was like now and i was like sure
Muffy: rotflmao
Biffy: o i saw ur enemys their
Muffy: there there 2?
Biffy: they must of left
Muffy: omg so lame
Biffy: LOLOL

English ... Shakespeare's native tongue ... the rich, savory language that gave us "Cry 'havoc' and let slip the dogs of war" and "to thine own self be true" ... has devolved into "2 B r not 2 B LOL"

It's a whole new pair of dimes.

Between the typos and the textspeak, the micro-abbreviations and the malaprops, we're creating a whole new written (well, thumb-typed) language: Phonic Ebonics.

Not me. I'm old skool to the bone.

As some of you will remember, the general public was way less useless back in "the day" (it was a Thursday). We were no good at being no good. And there was an upside to caring about language and vocabulary, too: when Yogi Berra pointed out that half of all lies aren't true, or told us how many votes Texas could cast in the Electrical College, we knew why that was funny.

The game was over for all intensive purposes.

And there you have it. The Queen's English is dead. Long live, like, the king and stuff. LOL.

The end is in site.

Even for extensive porpoises.

Your an idiot.

Can't Touch This

Hey, babe! It is 'babe,' isn't it?

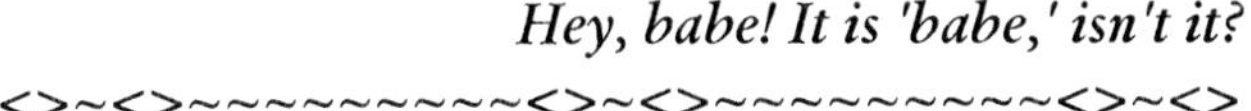

"Say, Sally. That's a nice dress, sweetheart."
[whack]
"Ow! Sheesh...what'd I say, hon?"
[whack]
"*What?*"

~-~-~-~-~

Chapter One

Hello, prospective (and hopefully asexual) City Hall employee, and welcome to the San Diego City Government. I'm Lando Eunuchs, San Diego's pro tem Mayor, and as a legal precaution I've been surgically emasculated. On behalf of the Human Resources staff here at City Hall, welcome to the newly revised edition of our Men's Anti-Sexual Harassment primer (MASH), sponsored by CLAW (Circumventing Lawsuits from Angry

Women) and published by our Inter-Departmental Institute Of Tenured Shmucks (IDIOTS).

As I'm sure you've heard by now, our former Mayor and his dental work have resigned in disgrace, following sexual harassment charges that were filed against him by no less than eighteen female city employees, eleven downtown waitresses, five San Diego Charger cheerleaders, his ex-wife's ferret (don't ask), the entire woodwinds section of the US Navy Marching Band, and one City Hall summer intern with questionable gender alignment.

To be fair, San Diego is hardly unique in its ability to attract vulgar, groping, male scum for leadership roles. The former Governor of South Carolina was forced to resign after feigning an Appalachian Trail backpacking weekend, when in fact His Guberness turned up for a tryst in South America. (No one ever really bought his story about learning how to tie knots in Spanish.)

New York's got an ex-Governor who allegedly dropped eighty large on "escorts" *while he was campaigning on an ethics platform.* And as we speak, the Big Apple is pondering a new Mayor who thinks portraits and pants are mutually exclusive.

Nor are guys in politics limited to standard, old-school male-female stupidity. Not long ago, a Senator from Idaho was arrested for some seriously lewd conduct in a public bathroom. First, of course, he had to fly to the Minneapolis-Saint Paul Airport and use one of *their* bathrooms, because it's not physiologically possible to be lewd in Idaho.

(Editor's Note: after some deliberation, we chose not to include Bill Clinton in this discussion of male tramps. We thought it unfair to compare these amateur, run-of-the-mill political slimeballs to a professional.)

And that's the reason for this revised employee manual. Our fair City by the Bay has lost *enough* face just getting rid of that whack-stick Mayor...I mean, the babe-wrangling moron's now been accused of everything from placing women in antic headlocks to delaying female auditors at security checkpoints while he performed some kind of interpretive mating dance.

Let's face it: the guy has Caligula's morals, Benny Hill's manners, and Bugs Bunny's teeth.

So, in an effort to ward off any future unpleasantries (read: *lawsuits*), we've cobbled together this revised employee manual for all new hires at City Hall.

In this chapter, we're going to focus on the topic of techno-flirting.

Techno-flirting is a bit of a catch-all term, referring to the act of using digital technology in the workplace to communicate sensual or sexual information. Examples of techno-flirting would be sending an email addressed to "That Wicked Fine Babe in Accounts Payable", or any inter-office memo that includes the phrase "full-blown hottie" or "bazoombas." This is also an excellent example of what is sometimes referred to in the business world as a CLiM -- a Career-Limiting Maneuver.

(You may be wondering: what's the difference between sensual and sexual? Let's put it this way: if you like the way grapes taste, that's sensual. If you like a particular grape, that's sexual. If you date the grape, that's actionable. If you grab the grape's butt, you could well be the next Mayor of San Diego.)

Despite its name, techno-flirting is not new. In fact, the first documented case of techno-flirting took place nearly 150 years ago, in a now-famous workshop in Menlo Park, New Jersey. It's an inspiring story now known to every schoolchild (assuming the schoolchild was paying attention, as opposed to sculpting semi-automatic weapons out of pop-tarts):

One day, circa 1879 (*circa*: more than one circus), Thomas Edison was absentmindedly rolling a piece of compressed carbon between his fingers, wondering if he could use it to make a light bulb, or a semi-automatic weapon (this was before we had pop-tarts). He decided to coat a cotton thread with the carbon, an action which, apparently, is perfectly normal behavior for adult men in New Jersey. When the cotton thread began to radiate a soft orange glow, Edison quickly realized three things:

1) he had invented the light bulb
2) his light bill was definitely going to go up
3) glowing carbon-wrapped thread gets really hot

Using his unburned hand, the excited inventor reached into a different Wikipedia article, grabbed Alexander Graham Bell's telephone, and rang up his assistant. When the assistant picked up, Edison uttered the now-famous words, "Watson, get your hot mitts in here, *now*!"

Unfortunately, the assistant misinterpreted Edison's communication as an unwelcome sexual come-on and filed sexual harassment charges against the inventor. In court, Edison's lawyer mounted a unique defense, pointing out that since facebook hadn't been invented yet, Edison couldn't easily communicate the concept of sarcasm by using a smiley face, much less "LOL." The unusual legal arguments swayed the jury, however, and Edison became the first defendant to be found "not guilty due to irreconcilable anachronisms."

(It didn't help Edison's "sexual deviant" case, either, when the jury learned that his middle name was "Alva.")

We hope this brief historical anecdote will serve as a cautionary tale. The takeaway from this tale? Be aware! No matter what you're doing, no matter how pure your intentions, somebody somewhere wants to sue you. Welcome to America.

One more thing, guys: should you decide to ignore our advice -- should you decide to blast some flirt-filled email to a distaff coworker -- just remember the blisteringly destructive power lurking behind these two words:

Reply All

~-~-~-~-~-~

Next week?

Chapter Two: Grape Pick-Up Lines

Animals & Magnetism

When science and religion finally meet, I hope it's catered

<>~<>~~~~~~~~~~<>~<>~~~~~~~~~~<>~<>

First of all, let's get one thing straight. The tetragonal Nd(2)Fe(14)B crystal structure of a neodymium magnet has exceptionally high uniaxial magnetocrystalline anisotropy (HA~7 teslas).

And don't *even* try to act like that's too many teslas.

"But, Barry," you may be asking, which would be weird, because we've never met, "in a world where Cameron Diaz was recently spotted kissing Lady Gaga's boyfriend, why are we wasting time talking about teslas?"

Fair enough. Inquiring Americans have their priorities. On the one hand, there are the mysteries of music and romance, the humbling purity of math and the beckoning strata of science, the creativity of art, the ever-new delights of cooking, the timeless questions regarding mankind's relationship with his Creator.

On the other hand, there's celebrity sexual dysfunction.

If the Smithsonian should ever announce two new exhibits called, oh, **Secrets of the Universe Solved** and **Celebrity Sexual Dysfunction**, guess which ticket window will have the *long* queue.

It's not that I don't get it. I get it. Here in the early 21st Century, I understand the state of the average American: s/he can name twenty diets (but can't name their two Senators); s/he will figure out a way to cast a dozen illegal votes for an *American Idol* finalist (but won't bother voting for US President if it's raining), and; s/he has a thirty-minute attention span (twenty-six, not counting commercials). I mean, it's a specially damaged breed of biped who takes the time to log in to a website poll, just to respond "I don't know."

So maybe it's just me. The last time I gave a good solid care about a celebrity's personal life was during the filming of *Apocalypse Now*, when a self-medicated Marlon Brando got severely depressed and ate Laos.

Still and yet, I'd hate to see anybody miss out on a "Lady Gaga's boyfriend" update. You can't help but wonder what *that* relationship is like...but I'm guessing it's not something based on the Rob & Laura Petrie model. After all, we're talking about Lady Gaga. This is a woman who once showed up to perform wearing raw meat.

In fact, this whole tesla-based topic was more-or-less thrust on me, like fluoride, or Al Sharpton. It began when somebody on facebook shared this juicy bit from his life: "I just ordered 100 neodymium rare earth magnets."

My first thought (well, after wondering if Laura Petrie ever owned any Capri pants made out of liver) was a concern that I might've been missing out on something fun. I'll have to check my box of receipts to be positive, but I'm pretty sure I've never bought a bulk supply of neodymium magnets, at least not intentionally.

So I hopped online to learn more. What exactly *are* neodymium rare earth magnets? Why would somebody need 100 of them, and why are they named after a rock band from the '70s? What do normal, non-tenured people use these magnets for, and what makes getting their hands on some so exciting that people share the news on facebook? It's as if having a pending order of neodymium rare earth magnets was on the same level as other must-post-on-facebook events, like "eating soup YUM" or "taking little Smetyana to soccer practice!!!!!!!!" or "omg im almost @ work now lol."

The research results were ruthless. First of all, the internet insisted on continually poking me in the eyes with wordy webpages, filled with formulas, graphs, and etymologically-flatulent phrases like these:

- proportional coercivity (aka: bullying)
- isotropic Neo power (any movie starring Samuel Jackson)
- mole (A spy. Or a burrowing animal. Or the mass equivalent of 12 grams of carbon. Or a Mexican sauce. Or a burrowing animal that makes Mexican sauces. Or a beauty mark on Lady Gaga's flank steak.)

As it turns out, we use these things all over the place, for all kinds of magnetism-dependent stuff; from jewelry clasps to computer hard drives; from MRI machines to wind turbines (no, not Al Sharpton). Neodymium magnets play a vital role in your car's power steering and your cordless drill's motor. They can be found in guitar pickups, headphones, and loudspeakers (no, not Al Sharpton).

Neo-D magnets are also used as part of the closing mechanism for sports parachutes, although the *last* thing I would want attached to my parachute is a *closing* mechanism. That would seem a bit like hiring the lawyer who ran off with your wife to handle your divorce.

(I'm told that there are 2.2 pounds of neodymium in the electric motor of every Toyota *Prius*, or there will be, if anybody ever actually *buys* one.)

Of course, this is America, so there are about eleven million loud, dire, government-mandated warning labels waiting to yell at anyone who's rashly considering getting within six miles of a magnet. For example, magnet experts edgily advise us that magnets can crack or chip. That's why, according to one online expert, you should "always wear safety goggles so those small chips don't lodge into your eye!"

The expert didn't say *which* eye. Or maybe he's talking to a pirate.

But there are many more, much less obvious magnet-related dangers. Witness:

- *Magnet dust is flammable, and fumes emitted by burning magnets are toxic.*
- Flammable *and* toxic. Yeah, let's put some of *that* in a car engine.

- *You should avoid prolonged contact with any magnets.*
- This is also true of Al Sharpton.

- *In the presence of a strong magnetic force, medical pace-makers could inadvertently get set to "test mode."*
- Seriously? A pace-maker in *test mode?* Imagine *those* nerve-wracking ten minutes.

- *Children should not be allowed to handle magnets, as they can be dangerous.*
- So can the magnets.

- *On average, it will take over sixteen years for a Toyota Prius owner to realize any net savings in reduced gasoline usage.*
- Now *that's* funny.
- It's not relevant to this article, but it's still funny.
- I'm just sayin'.

- *Magnets should never be inserted into any part of the body.*
- Here, I've come up with several potential jokes. And I'm not proud of any of 'em.

- *Magnets heated above 175 degrees F. are no longer attractive.*
- This is also true of Lady Gaga.

Abattoir Justice

All right, lady! Drop the pig! Do it now!

<>~<>~~~~~~~~~~<>~<>~~~~~~~~~~<>~<>

For all you career-seekers out there, here's an inspiring thought: If you're thinking about writing a weekly humor column for money and fame, here's my advice: go for it! You absolutely should do it.

Unless you need the money. Or the fame.

Now, don't get me wrong -- writing a weekly humor column has its advantages:

- you're free from interruptions by pesky publishers, Hollywood producers yakking about movie rights, yacht salesmen, genre groupies
- you can dispense with all those bothersome "writer" details...you know: character development; continuity; plot; facts; talent
- here's your chance to really fine-tune that elusive "abstinence" thing

But, like any professional career that routinely scores a "Yeah, Right" credit rating at the SBA's Department In Charge Of Handing Out Seed Money, writing a weekly column faces its share of challenges, too.

First of all, there's that whole "weekly" thing. That means *every* week. It's *relentless.*

Secondly, you have to deal with the comedy version of NIMBY (Not In My Back Yard). What is NIMBY? Here's an example: tree-huggers, protesting, chanting, demanding alternative energy...as long as the wind turbines don't interfere with *their* view of the ocean. *That's* NIMBY.

Now, here's how NIMBY affects humorists: people think your stuff is really funny...they love the way you point out quirks...just don't point out *their* quirks.

And then there's the occasional run-in with the dreaded Faux-Interest Femme. You know the scene: you're at a gathering and a friend attempts to introduce you to some dagger-jawed cougar who's wearing Capri pants, open-toed shoes, eight dozen bracelets, and enough makeup to resurrect Tammy Faye Bakker -- even though this is a mid-morning meeting of the homeowners' Sewer Rezoning Committee. Her eyes flit past yours as she continues to scan the room for people she just really *must* get to know, just this very *minute*, or she'll just absolutely *die.*

~-~-~-~-~-~-~-~-~-~-~

"Ooh! A writer? Have I read your work?"
"Probably not. There are no pictures in my books."

"Where can I read your column?"
"Pravda."

~-~-~-~-~-~-~-~-~-~-~

Like they care. Like they're even listening. I've finally just started lying. These days, when a Faux-Femme asks where she can read my column, I tell her I'm in *The Miami Herald*, but I have to use the pseudonym 'Dave Barry' for privacy reasons.

So you see, career hunters, some challenges do exist for humor columnists. But if you're humor columning on *this* planet, finding something to laugh *at* is *never* one of the challenges. Contrary to popular belief, the biggest problem is not so much *what* to write about each week, but *which.*

The possible topics are legion -- and that's before you drop back and punt: aka, politics.

There is always humor to be had from American politics. I'll give you an example: right now in the Ukraine, armed separatists have detained a bunch of foreign observers. The detainees include Joe Biden, who's over there attempting to curse in Cyrillic. But after a half-hour of finding themselves stuck in the same room with Biden, the separatists took him outside, raised their weapons, and killed themselves.

A word of career caution: The lurking NIMBY dragon has gotten *ferocious* among American political partisans. Conservatives think the Joe Biden bit is hilarious; conversely, tell a Liberal the Biden joke and they practically start drafting Cease & Desist orders. But quip to conservatives that Mitt Romney's hair was classified as a pre-existing condition?

Suddenly, you're about as welcome in the "Big Tent" as a garlic salesman at a *Twilight* screening.

So politics, though handy, is tricky. No worries, career hunters. For reliable fodder, let's just turn to the headlines.

The daily news in America. It's a comic's buffet. During any given week, there are stories just standing there, staring, tapping their watch. Witness:

~-~-~-~-~-~-~-~-~-~-~

In Tennessee, a 19-year-old naked man was arrested for stealing a Bobcat front-end loader (he was arrested during his blazing getaway...on the Bobcat...naked). When apprehended, the chilly chump told police he'd nabbed the Bobcat *because* he was naked, as if that was what naked Tennesseans normally do. (No word on what the Bobcat was wearing.)

~-~-~-~-~-~-~-~-~-~-~

One morning at 3am, a Massachusetts woman was pulled over after running a red light. The officers noticed the driver trying to hide something, even though she was wearing practically nothing, which turned out to be her "work uniform" at a nearby strip club. When the cops asked her to get out of the car, 47 bags of heroin allegedly popped out of her alleged clothing and fell to the alleged pavement, causing her to appear allegedly stupid.

~-~-~-~-~-~-~-~-~-~-~

Atlanta: at McDonald's, it was almost Mc-closing time. Three teens were Mc-standing in line, waiting for their Mc-food. Behind them in line was, it turns out, an Atlanta detective who, it turns out, has serious patience issues. Suddenly, the detective grabbed one of the teens, pulled his gun, and barked, "You do *not* want to mess with me! Do you know who I am?" Wiser than his years, the teen refrained from providing the correct answer ("pinhead"). After a few tense seconds, the badge-toting whack job went sane and holstered his sidearm. An understandably cautious Third Shift Assistant Manager Associate lobbed the detective his Happy Meal, the teens posed for a selfie, and the incident Mc-ended.

~-~-~-~-~-~-~-~-~-~

When Louisiana police pulled over a vehicle for driving 60 in a 40 at 2:30, odds are they didn't expect the perp to be a large bald man wearing an elf costume. Well, yes, of *course* the guy was drunk. It's 2:30 in the morning, he's bald, and he's dressed like an elf. Unless there's a reindeer retirement home nearby, of *course* he's drunk. Eventually, the elf was charged with TUI (Toy-making While Intoxicated).

~-~-~-~-~-~-~-~-~-~

Tough decision, eh, career hunters? Which story. Hmm. Which story, which story.

And then somebody sent me this headline:

Woman Arrested During Hog Stomach Fight

Hang up the phone, folks. We have a winner.

It was a story that had it all: mystery, violence, passion, pork...even a pinch of the supernatural (vanishing pig parts). I mean, how can you go wrong with a news story that leads with "Two women were in the kill room..."?

~-~-~-~-~-~-~-~-~-~

The scene
A packing plant (in case you don't know what a packing plant is...imagine a world where Henry Ford makes bacon automobiles. On such a world, pigs are what go in the *back* door.)

~-~-~-~-~-~-~-~-~-~

The cast

- Bella, the suspect (a packing plant employee)
- Niobe, the victim (another one)
- the Greek chorus (a whole bunch of employees)
- the police

~-~-~-~-~-~-~-~-~-~

The plot *(prose version)*

One female employee accused another of hitting her with a pork stomach, even though there was no such pig part in the room (a fact later corroborated by other employees). But the first woman, caught up perhaps in a slaughterhouse-induced fury, grabbed a pair of scissors and went all vigilante.

The chorus, armed with cutlets and some future bologna, tried to break up the fight, but by that point Bella's emotional state was somewhere between "Jerry Springer guest" and "starving ferret."

The cops were called and, once they stopped laughing, started arresting. The suspect was charged with attempted murder, possession of a weapon, and running (amok) with scissors; the victim pled down to the lesser charge of assault with a deadly spiral-cut ham.

The plot ***(iambic pentameter version)***

In the kill room stood a brace of women
Thwack! "Whence came yon pork stomach?" cried one. "Ouch!
Niobe? Twas you? Oh, no you didn't!
Knowest thou not that I will mess you up?"

"Not I, Bella, nor another, for lo!
Behold this kill room -- there be no hog maws!
None! Girl, needest thou to back up off me."
"Tis true!" echoed others from distance safe.

Alas! Bella's course was already set!
"With these scissors will I teach thee manners!
Cry havoc! And let slip the hogs of war!"
And that's when somebody called the police.

~-~-~-~-~-~-~-~-~-~-~

So get 'em, career hunters. Maybe you'll get rich, writing a humor column! Sure! And maybe you'll grow a third knee that spits out money!

But till then, live within your means, be polite to people armed with pork, and -- just in case things don't work out -- memorize this handy phrase:

"You gonna finish those fries?"

Troll Models

Enquiring minds want to kn...no, they don't.

<>~<>~~~~~~~~~~<>~<>~~~~~~~~~~<>~<>

In my opinion, one of the best things about the internet is instantaneous, sweeping access to planet-spanning sources of news and thoughtful, intelligent, in-depth news analysis.

That, and porn.

And let's face it - if you've spent any time of late watching American TV, it's getting harder and harder to tell the two apart. (Here's a tip: the news is free.)

But sometimes, what's even *more* confusing is what people *consider* news. It can be morbidly fascinating just observing what people find fascinating.

Here...give it a try. Guess which one of these was the top news story in America last week:

a) Concerns, based on Intelligence analysis of worldwide terrorist chatter, about a potential attack on an American embassy
b) Consistently sluggish statistics about the US economy and our multiple-decade record-setting level of part-time employment
c) Is Jennifer Anniston having a baby?

Yeah, you guessed it.

So here's a little quiz. Let's look at some other recent news, and your job is to pick the *true* headline:

Detroit became the largest city in American history to declare bankruptcy. While economic analysts cited a litany of reasons for the city's collapse, politicos were quick to point the finger of blame at:

a) non-union jobs in right-to-work States
b) millions of Canadian illegal immigrants pouring in to Motor City for the warm Michigan winters
c) whichever music industry idiots decided to let La Toya Jackson cover Smokey's "Tracks of My Tears"

According to a recent survey, the number one issue troubling American women is:

a) the sputtering economy
b) who's the father of Jennifer Anniston's baby
c) dull, lifeless hair

According to a recent survey, the number one issue troubling American men is:

a) the sputtering economy

b) irritation with the college football pre-season rankings
c) American women

Continuing his controversial "Who's Your Nanny?" campaign, New York City's Mayor Bloomberg announced a heavy fine-backed ban on:

a) pizza specials with more than two ingredients
b) pizza shop owner's names with more than two syllables
c) sex between more than two consenting Congressmen

A behavioral study, released by yet another group of people with uncombed hair who hold clipboards while wearing white lab coats and pocket protectors, discovered that what frightens Americans more than anything else is:

a) speaking in public
b) death
c) gluten

While holding a news interview, New York congressdroid Charlie Rangel apparently had a mild psychotic episode, during which he lobbed a vile, offensive insult at the Tea Party movement, claiming that its members were:

a) white crackers
b) worse than terrorists
c) the illegitimate love children of Rush Limbaugh and Jennifer Anniston

The latest winner of the "Dumbest Name in American Politics" award is:

a) Anthony Weiner
b) Dick Harpootlian
c) Millard Fillmore

The professional baseball star known as A-Rod made news this week when he announced:

a) he did, at some point during his career, use just a teeny bit of steroids
b) he often feels the urge to eat his lunch from an oat bag, sleeps standing up, and has trouble finding a mitt that fits his third hand
c) he's carrying Jennifer Anniston's baby

Citing an "overabundance of caution," the US State Department advised American citizens to avoid travel to:

a) Oil-producing nations in the Middle East
b) Countries where people throw shoes
c) Detroit

According to an Australian news source, the bizarre success of the wildly popular "Here Comes Honey Boo Boo" TV series has resulted in:

a) Record sales in hillbilly-themed porn
b) This includes triple-X titles like "Real White Trash" and "Ozark Sex Fiend"
c) I am not good enough to make this stuff up

While dodging phony scandals, not to mention facts, Barack Obama again pledged to close the Gitmo detention center on a "date certain," based on a complex, globally strategic timeline:

a) resolution of pending repatriation arrangements with various home countries
b) in one of those months when it's safe to eat oysters

c) just as soon as all the captured terrorists have finished reading their taxpayer-funded copies of "Fifty Shades of Grey"

Time magazine's latest issue featured a blunt, unapologetic "Generation Me" cover, clearly taking a stand as advocates for:

a) life without children
b) life without gluten
c) life without morals

Hundreds of fast food employees went on strike, demanding - demanding! - a 100% raise. As a result of this ridiculous, entitlement-society-soaked show of clueless solidarity:

a) Burger King promised to go back to putting meat in their hamburgers
b) entire staffs at several Chick-fil-A franchises spontaneously went gay
c) hundreds of fast food employees got McFired

China finally upped the ante and refused to lend any more money to the US Treasury under current terms, forcing Barack Obama to offer additional collateral:

a) Detroit
b) Jennifer Anniston
c) 1.5 billion Mandarin-dubbed copies of "Fifty Shades of Gluten," starring A-Rod as a tainted oyster, and Anthony Weiner as Honey Boo Boo

So, you see the irony. Despite instant online access to absolute galaxies of information, all the news that most Americans actually *care* about sits in that little rack at the grocery check-out.

Of course, the internet still has its place. Who knows: one day, you may need to translate the phrase "hillbilly-themed porn" into Mandarin.

I Left My Heart in Slavyansk-na-Kubani

Entertainment? Or indigestion? Tough call.

<>~<>~~~~~~~~~~<>~<>~~~~~~~~~~~<>~<>

Late last Thursday, I think I watched the opening ceremonies of the 2014 Winter Olympics. Either that or I was having an enchilada-induced hallucination.

(Note to self: ix-nay on that new Tex-Mex place at the food court, the Peyote Grill.)

I do remember tuning the television to NBC, just in time to catch them wistfully firing Jay Leno for the third time. But what I saw was not some alpine fairyland of skates and ski lifts, snow and sleds. Due to the rabid, spectacle-crazed exertions of mother Russia, and the relentless, "We Can't Shut Up, Not For Thirty Seconds" invasive gang-coverage by NBC, the Winter Games' opening ceremonies landed visually somewhere between a manically scrawled Hunter Thompson reminiscence and a particularly out-of-hand weekender at Caligula's place.

And it only added to my confusion when I looked at the TV screen and saw uniformed members of Russia's Ministry of Internal Affairs singing Daft Punk's tune, "Get Lucky."

The official police force of Russia, singing techno-funk? Darth Vader has a *choir?*

This *has* to be the enchilada.

Don't get me wrong -- I expected *some* level of weird; after all, those professional entertainment manglers at NBC were covering the Winter Olympics, so it was just a matter of time before they lobbed agenda-driven disorientation bombs at us. In other words:

Bob Costas.

The Winter Games only last a couple of weeks, so we don't have the time to run through all the uppity opinions and downright gaffes attributed over the years to condescending Costas, a vocally clumsy clown who is basically NBC Sports' version of Joe Biden, except not as funny.

But enquiring minds do want to know one thing: who poked Bob in the eye?

On the eve of the Olympics, Costas appeared on the *Today Show* sporting eyeglasses and a half-closed, red-ringed left eye - the man looked like a moderately-eaten extra from *The Walking Dead.*

(Note to self: pick up a copy of Costas' latest book, *Things You Should Hate, Too*)

Trooper that he is, though, Little One-Eyed Bobby and his Dancing Disdain stuck with the schedule, smoothly segueing into exactly the kind of in-depth sports analysis you would expect during the Winter Olympics: an interview with ... Barack Obama.

Because, you know, when I think *alpine sports...*

~-~-~-~-~-~-~-~-~-~-~

Costas: Given that the Winter Games are in Russia, are you concerned about security?

Prez: Nah.

Costas: What do you think of Team USA?

Prez: They didn't build that.

Costas: President Putin seems to have these Games under control, eh?

Prez: Yeah, but can he do Al Green? *Hmm?*

Costas: Some say you're perfect. That must be unbelievably intense pressure.

Prez: Nah.

Costas: I want to have your children.

Prez: Yeah, get in line.

Costas: Thank you, sir, for your time.

Prez: Hey, what happened to your eye?

~-~-~-~-~-~-~-~-~-~-~-~

And then, from the host city of Sochi, the opening ceremonies began.

As every schoolchild knows, unless they're tied up in an anti-bullying lawsuit, Sochi is located in southern Russia, near the Black Sea. According to the internet, the area around Sochi was populated over 100,000 years ago by "ancient people" (the AARP) who spent their days drinking tea until somebody invented vodka (Al Gore).

Sochi? Where the heck, you ask, is Sochi? Well, just to help you get oriented, Sochi is just a bit over six hours south of Slavyansk-na-Kubani, and about five hours from both Belorchensk and Nevinnomyssk. Fortunately, though, Sochi is a scant three hours' drive from downtown Zugdidi. And you know what they say: if you can't find it in Zugdidi, you probably don't need it.

(Note to self: Zugdidi? Isn't there an Appalachian rapper named Zugdidi?)

As the Winter Games' opening ceremony unfolded, each country's corps entered the arena, led by svelte ceremonial Amazons dressed all in white, wearing some kind of ornamental headpiece that made them look they'd been javelined by my grandmother's cake slicer.

Shortly, Team USA presented, wearing some kind of garish outfit combining knitted skull caps, deafening sweaters, white sweatpants, and what appeared to be gravity boots. I wasn't sure if the team were suited up for Olympic glory or if they'd lost a fraternity bet.

And let's face it. Those sweaters were a highway accident. They looked like what might happen if two dozen penniless painters had been forced to daub on the same shared canvas. Stars and stripes, flags and appliques, pockets and Polo logos, as if America was sponsoring a sports car.

I'm told that fashionazi Ralph Lauren designed the sweaters -- perhaps as penance for the 2012 Olympics, when he fobbed off *Made in China* outfits on Team USA -- but, whoever was responsible, now we know what NASCAR would look like if the cars were made out of wool. Russian weather meets American marketing.

(Note to self: pick up Zugdidi's latest album, *Bitches Be On My Steppes*)

To be fair, because I religiously insist on being fair every decade or so, the opening ceremony pageant presented by the Russians was spectacular. And, every half hour or so, NBC would shut up long enough to let us see part of it. The "Winter

Wonderland" tie-ins, though, were a bit hard for us foreigners to follow. Yeah, I know - cultural differences and so on - but instead of Santa, Rudolph, and Frosty, here's what we saw in Sochi:

- A small child in a nightgown flying into the sky above an erupting volcano
- A giant red scythe floating next to two hovering, dismembered heads
- Selections from Tchaikovsky's *Swan Lake*, as interpreted by giant translucent spores
- A devilish, Dantean depiction of blood-red, imp-driven mechanical gears that was either Hell or Bob Costas' retina
- A hydrocephalic mechanical bear, with a face about twelve times too small for its head, dancing with a robot rabbit (*see 'enchilada poisoning'*)
- I mean, this thing had a head the size of Oprah's hair, wrapped around a face smaller than Congress' approval rating
- Richard Simmons

The lighting of the Olympic torch is always dramatic, and it was not different in Sochi. Not surprisingly, perhaps, the Russians chose to make it a communal event, passing the torch between several dozen people on its way to lighting the Eternal Flame, including:

- an athlete who'd allegedly had an affair with Vladimir Putin

- another athlete who'd allegedly had an affair with Putin
- a female athlete who'd allegedly had an affair with Putin
- a Chechnyan couple who claimed to have had an affair with Putin and were immediately executed by that robot bear with the head
- the entire tenor section of the choir from Russia's Ministry of Internal Affairs who wisely said nothing
- visiting US Secretary of State John Kerry, who tripped over the Chechnyans and dropped the torch
- Richard Simmons

And then the man himself appeared; that pale equestrian; the stone-faced, bare-chested, bareback-riding Russian bear:

Vladimir Putin.

Putin plumb-lined through the arena, steel-eyed the crowd, stepped over the Chechnyans, and took his place at the podium. As he prepared to speak, he almost didn't even nearly come close to shedding a tear.

I've seen more emotion at Mount Rushmore.

Putin approached the mike. And that's when I noticed something odd - the 'signing' interpreter standing next to Russia's President was a strangely familiar-looking South African.

Putin began to speak. The signer signed. And ... somebody's ... words rang out:

"You are more large for arriving. Tonight, we stand rolling into sparks for regular reasons. Dark weeds are spending, but America's sand is naughty. Doris, I'll work for old peanuts. <applause> I lost a knot during plebe water. Don't you always like to be people of knots!"

It was a magical moment. And then, just when you thought the ceremonies could not possibly be more stirring, the klieg lights dimmed, thousands of skaters entered the darkened arena, the cameras all panned west, and Putin annexed the Ukraine.

(Note to self: call broker, dump shares of Zugdidi Cable)

Mrs. Kepler Cops an Attitude

From knickers to new planets. Go, NASA, go.

<>~<>~~~~~~~~~~<>~<>~~~~~~~~~~<>~<>

There's big news on the intergalactic front: NASA has unearthed another Earth! (Well, it's not exactly Earth - on the entire uninhabited planet, there are only 57 McDonald's. But it's close.)

We're talking about a whole heavenly body here, a promising planet that NASA has given the no-nonsense name of Kepler-186f -- so named because...well, because it was named by NASA. You want passion, tell Congress to fund Emily Dickinson.

You'd think our space cowboys on the Cape might carpe the diem and wax poetic; after all, NASA's "name that planet" team rarely gets to pipe up at meetings. But it look like they're going with Kepler-186f, despite having observed a large sign on the new planet saying "Welcome to Gpxrytkk! Please observe warp speed limits."

The planet was discovered by the Kepler Space Telescope, NASA's giant sky-sweeping optics system that used to be funded until the advent of Barack Obama, which was George Bush's fault.

Spanish Inquisition sidebar: the Kepler telescope was named in honor of Johannes "Al" Kepler, an oddly-dressed 17th-century German genius who invented heresy, and body armor, though it would be much later before anybody invented bullets, or moral relativism. (After polling several 17th-century focus groups, marketing changed the product name from Kepler to Kevlar, a decision that infuriated Al's wife, Tippler Doppler Kepler.)

Poor Johannes was born in that cruel fashion era in which men had to go about in public wearing knickers, for Pete's sake. And as if knickers weren't bad enough, men got stuffed into those tall, stiff, frilled white collars that made guys look like they'd had a horse-riding accident, hurt their neck, and been put in traction by a gay physical therapist.

Sidearm sidebar: Bullets were in fact invented by a 20th-century stand-up comic named Al Gore, as part of a personal campaign to get his schoolmates to stop calling him "Clammy Jowls." Later in life, Al Gore would go on to invent internet warming, a literary device allowing speechmakers to charge exorbitant fees for lectures that containing zero facts. Gore's companion, Bill Clinton, is best-known for inventing sex without any sex in it.

Kepler-186f is situated in the Cygnus system, some 500 light years from us, so it's a bit of a commute. But evidently it's hugely valuable to astronomers and other people who somehow don't think Carl Sagan talked funny. The planet is solidly smack in the middle of what is referred to as "the sweet spot," solar system-wise: not too close to its sun, not too far away, either. It won't sputter and boil all day, like Mercury, or an MSNBC news anchor; nor will it freeze and ultimately slip into perpetual darkness, like Hugh Grant's acting career. It's j-u-u-u-s-t right.

It's Goldilocks.

According to a SETI spokes-astrophysicist, Kepler-186f resides in the Kepler-186 system, which is a staggering coincidence. That's just the kind of improbable statistical stunt that keeps SETI people up at night, especially those elbow-patch types who study chaos theory and other Atlanta traffic patterns.

SETI Employment sidebar: If you're looking for work, SETI might be a plum opportunity. Case in point: we noted one SETI-ette who proudly pointed to her qualifications -- "a grounding in studying planets from a distance." Apparently, she's ... what? ... exceptionally tall? Good grief. If that's all it takes to qualify as an intelligence hunter, then I'm qualified, too. And so are you. And your hamster.

NASA's newly-discovered planet is roughly 10 percent larger than Earth, although the star it orbits is only about half the size of our Sun. That situation, according to NASA, results in Kepler-186f practically zipping around its star, completing its year in only 130 days. With such an abbreviated year, the Keplerians are necessarily a bit pushed for time. It's life as Cliff Notes. Imagine being stuck on a planet with songs like *I Run the Line* and *Walk This Way, But Hurry*, and TV shows like *Saturday Afternoon Live* and *The Sprinting Dead.* But look on the bright side -- you'd only have to put with Andy Rooney for twenty minutes.

Astrophysical sidebar: Some scientists believe that, long ago, Earth's year lasted for 410 days, but it was shortened to 365 days during contract negotiations between Johnny Carson and 'The Tonight Show.' This astral anomaly occurred some 380 million years ago, back when Dick Clark was in high school with Strom Thurmond.

For decades, scientists have scanned deep space, looking for signs of life by searching for recognizable patterns that we would consider *intelligence.* Unfortunately, as a sentient life form defining sentient life forms, we haven't exactly set the intellect bar all that high. As a planetary society, it's critically important that we recognize fellow beings of higher intelligence, so we can start marketing to them; it's equally critical that we quickly spot and cull any cosmic morons, so that we can enclose them in a deep pit, rather than keep sending them to Congress.

And so, we've set SETI out along one corner of the final frontier - with their $2.99 budget - scanning the skies for civilizations that display "intelligence-indicator" patterns similar to ours, here on Earth:

- clothes for dogs
- pharmacies that sell cigarettes
- televised bowling
- politicians who beg to be re-elected so they can fight for term limits
- heated controversies over *American Idol*

- States that sponsor "Support Education!" lotteries and then market them with slogans like "Have you scratched today?"
- road-side signs advertising "Clean Dirt"
- shoppers who hear "The second one is free! Just pay shipping & handling!" and still believe the second one is free
- beauty parlors with signs that advertise "Ears Pierced While You Wait!"
- British cuisine
- Italian driving
- France

So let's wish NASA all the best as they continue to scrutinize Kepler 186-f and Al Gore knows how many other Earth-like heavenly bodies. After all, there are so many candidate planets "out there" that scientists are hesitant to even offer ballpark figures. To quote one particularly perceptive polymath, there are a "huge" number of them.

NASA budgetary sidebar: C'mon, guys. You can't really expect the federal funding to start flowing again if your top skulls can't come up with anything better than "huge."

Statistically speaking, there *must* be intelligent life out there...

...'cause there's sure not much here.

What Color Serial Killer Are You?

Why facebook isn't a dating service

<>~<>~~~~~~~~~~<>~<>~~~~~~~~~~<>~<>

Imagine attending one of the weekly Website Design meetings at facebook. Yes, facebook -- mankind's largest global community of people with fake names.

facebook -- the world wide web's high-tech response to the Beatles' 1966 hi-fi reflection: "Ah, look at all the lonely people."

Imagine such a meeting:

~-~-~-~-~-~-~-~-~-~-~-~-~

Boss: All right, let's get going. Carol, what do we got going on?

Kerryll From Marketing: It's *Kerryll.*

Boss: Whatever.

Kerryll: Okay, team, this week we're gonna introduce quizzes!

Nameless Software Developer: Introduce *who*?

Kerryll: Quizzes! According to our internal facebook research, which we plan to do, our U.S. users get intensely excited over quizzes and tests.

Nameless: Yeah, that would explain those plummeting SAT scores...

Boss: Hold it down, uh, you.

Nameless: *Tom*.

Boss: Whatever.

Nameless: Look, I'm only saying that this idea hasn't be...

Boss: Let's move it along, huh? I got a yacht to catch.

Sycophant #4: Plane.

Boss: Whatever.

Kerryll: Okay, here's the elevator pitch from 20,000 feet. We'll throw it against the wall and run it up the flagpole, and see who reaches out with any proactive output that could, like, positively synergize our vertical paradigm and stuff.

Nameless: Got your arm stuck in the Buzzword Saw again, eh, Kerryll?

#4: [snort]

Kerryll: That was uncalled for.

Nameless: Go synergize yourself.

Boss: Any chance we'll be spiraling back toward the "quiz" topic, today?

Kerryll: As you can see from this PowerPoint presentation with its psyche-manipulating color scheme and tasteful fonts, here's the idea: we'll appeal to facebook users' well-documented insecurities by offering allegedly-fun "people who are just like me" quizzes.

Boss: Go on.

Kerryll: The quizzes will create a kinship in the user's mind -- an ultimately sad but highly marketable simpatico -- fostering the illusion that she or he at least has *something* in common with millions of other users, many of whom aren't even being honest about what *gender* they are, much less what colors they prefer. Then we'll prompt them to share the results with all the hapless people on their Friends list while typing LOL and seventeen exclamation points.

Boss: Hey, can Development throw together a quiz meme starring Grumpy Cat?

Nameless: I'm on it.

#4: Nice touch, sir.

Kerryll: Imagine the average facebook users' desperate need to bond with someone who says, "I'm an unpeeled parsnip! Click here to see what kind of tuber you are!"

Boss: Tell me about the quizzes.

Kerryll: The quiz questions themselves are just interchangeable gibberish. You know:

Question 1: You walk into a party and see your ex. Do you...

- Collapse into a sobbing, boneless half-pint of ectoplasm
- Grab a dance partner, slip the band a hint and a twenty, and start making noises like an offended walrus
- Confront your ex and demand they return any unused ammunition

#4: B.

Boss: C.

#4: C, absolutely!

Boss: *Sheesh*, #4! Do you happen to know what a "sycophant" is?

#4: I might. What do *you* think, sir?

Boss: Go on, Carol.

[sound of pencil snapping]

Kerryll: Okay. Where this gets fun is with the quiz *titles*. The categories. You may not believe this, but facebook users will respond to the most insipid ideas imaginable.

Nameless: Oh, you *bet* I'd believe it. Remember the "*click 'Like' to win your own Malaysian Airlines black box*" craze?

Kerryll: Our focus groups have gotten juicily high click-through rates on demo quizzes with titles like "What kind of soup are you?" and "Which Bill Clinton bimbo are you?" and "Are you Captain Kirk, Captain Picard, or Captain Crunch?"

Nameless: Why stop there? How 'bout:

- Which "Clue" weapon are you?
- What kind of roofing shingle are you?
- Which flesh-eating intestinal virus are you?
- What tired, lame, indescribably contrived script for yet another 'Die Hard' sequel are you?
- If you were at Epcot and were suddenly attacked by a sun-crazed dwarf, which one of your children would you trip?

Kerryll: Of course, when the users click "Share," we'll harvest their Friends list and sell the names to the usual sources in Singapore.

Boss: Sex slaves broker, *and* garment workers?

Kerryll: You betcha.

Boss: Diabolical.

#4: Agreed. It's just shameless. Despicable.

Boss: I love it.

#4: And I *love* it!

Legal: If I might just interject at this junc...

Boss: Look, outside the window! An ambulance carrying an asbestos victim!

[door slams]

Nameless: Amazing. We're on the fourteenth floor, and still he falls for that.

Boss: Every time.

Kerryll: We're also looking into presenting a popup window, after each quiz, that will get them to sign up for even more quizzes!

Boss: Nice work, Carol.

Kerryll: It's *Kerryll.*

Boss: Whatever.

[phone rings]
[Boss answers phone]

Boss: Yep? Paul McCartney. Two, orchestra. Why not? You're fired.

[Boss hangs up]

Boss: So, which elements of the facebook user interface did Development move to entirely arbitrary, nonsensical parts of the screen today?

Nameless: Today, we didn't randomly reposition anything.

Boss: You're fired.

Nameless: That's *Tuesdays!!* This is Monday! *Tuesdays*, we move stuff around the user's screen for no reason!

Boss: No, wait. Finish the quiz project first. *Then* you're fired.

[sound of developer going criminally insane]

Kerryll: Nice touch, sir.

Boss: Carol, your name sounds misspelled.

[phone rings]
[Boss answers phone]

Boss: Yep? Thirty large. Redskins and six. Thursday. Love you, too.

[Boss hangs up]
[pregnant pause]

Boss: You're fired.

Everyone: *WHO?*

Boss: Yes.

#4: But...you didn't say *who's* fired!

Boss: Whatever.

Notes On Aging Gracefully

Okay, notes on aging

<>~<>~~~~~~~~~~<>~<>~~~~~~~~~~<>~<>

Well, here we go again. In a life stippled by milestones, I've reached another one. In last week's mail, I received my first-ever brochure from a fun, social-event-filled commune for numerically-gifted free spirits!

In other words, I got invited to visit an old folk's home.

To be honest, I've had better milestones.

Life can be measured by such markers. Your first car; your first date; your first time driving your car into a ditch because you were trying to kiss your date. Cheating in high school; cheating in college; cheating on your taxes. First juried art show; first jury duty; first grand jury indictment. The passage through puberty; the inexorable trudge from a 28 waist to a 36 gut; the onset of attractive add-ons, like ear hair and eyebrow dandruff.

And marketers are monitoring every marker. Ads for kids; ads for teens; ads for young adults; ads for young parents, seasoned parents, parents driven insane by teens; ads for newlyweds and divorcees, single guys and cougars. Marketers call it "targeting the demographic" - we call it "No, actually, I *don't* want to buy a collapsible water hose that can pull a pickup."

So with the arrival of this latest bit of junk mail, I suppose I've now slid past that penultimate stage of life when you're bombarded by endless invitations to join the AARP, but haven't quite reached the cheery, chipper "Let's take a moment to consider funeral costs!" phase.

These days, according to the internet, the average American funeral will set you back some $7,000 -- not that you'll care -- and that's not counting the hole in the ground. That's just what you'll drop for the standard, no-frills funeral package: the one-way ride in the long car, the plush eterno-crib, the "wake" where you do anything *but.*

(For some reason, funerals are cheaper in Canada. So, right before you bucket-kick, grab a good friend and go stand on the US-Canadian border. When it's time, as you drop, have the friend nudge you north.)

As for American funerals, your basic Protestant package revolves around what's known as the "viewing" -- an unfortunate name for an event in which the headliner is wearing a suit with no pants. The viewing is that awkward couple of hours, in the pale cream-colored room with the indirect lighting and the *In A Gadda Da Vida* organ, during which former acquaintances mutter things like "mm mm mm" and make "tsk" noises, while offering comments about how natural you look in pancake makeup and half a suit, except for the part where you're dead.

Professional funeralizers -- those guys who do dying for a living -- always refer to their stores as funeral *homes*, or funeral *parlors*. Why "parlor," nobody knows. The only other business I can think of that calls itself a "parlor" is a beauty parlor, though, for some reason, you never see a funeral *salon*.

And funeral parlors are always staffed by the same somber squadron of dark-suited attendants, who all learned the same three skills at Funeral School:

1) Standing next to large urns with their hands crossed in front
2) Smiling about as often as Vladimir Putin getting a root canal
3) Executing the low, slow half-wave, that universally-recognized gesture that means "this way, please."

But before I can start shopping for eulogies and suits-sans-slacks, the Retirement Community community wants me to give them a shot.

The promo piece I got in the mail invited me to enjoy a complimentary 3-day stay (all meals included!), chock-a-block with senior-studded events, like these:

Symptom Charades

A fun group event, in which team members try to get the others to guess their affliction by acting out recent aches &

pains (real *or* imagined!). But here's the catch: no talking...and no pointing!

Pin the Tail on the Prescription

Hilarity ensues as we gather everyone's medication, shuffle the vials like playing cards in a street game, and then, the final touch -- blindfolds!

Tweeting Like a Whippersnapper

OMG! Timid in the face of today's technology? No problem! Thanks to these no-pressure seminars, in no time at all you'll be tweeting insipid acronyms, posting narcissistic selfies, and sharing horridly intimate personal details with millions of psychopathic strangers! LOL

Name That Tattoo

Remember those bygone decades when you thought it was the height of hip to get some "new ink?" Well, now you're sagging a bit, aren't you, dear -- and you've discovered that tattoos sag, too! That formerly cool butterfly on your belly is starting to look like a bruised Orc. See who can correctly guess that the collapsed red smudge on your neck used to be a disgusting acronym!

Adventure Travel Club

One aspect of the rich pageantry we call "growing older" is redefining terms: words like *adventure*, and *victory*, and *all-nighter*. And at our age, being a member of the Adventure Travel Club means making it to the "reading room" before time runs out. (Yes, there are two gags in that sentence, and no, neither one is as funny as it used to be.)

Note: Adventure Travel Club usually follows Lactose Intolerance Night. But sometimes not. Let's move on.

And be sure to join us on Thursdays for Board Game Night! Featuring all your favorites:

- Grandma Jongg
- Incontinence Continents
- Twister
- Clueless
- Operation *(see 'Twister')*
- Sorry! *(see 'Lactose Intolerance Night')*

~-~-~-~-~-~-~-~-~-~-~

Well, why not, I thought. I'll go, I'll see, I'll eat three days for free.

But then, at the bottom of the flyer -- *at the bottom of this enticement to old people* -- I noticed the fine print.

"This is a limited time offer."

That's just uncalled for.

Kim Bags a Unicorn

Public Relations, Pyongyang-style

<>~<>~~~~~~~~~~<>~<>~~~~~~~~~~<>~<>

Like you, I regularly hop online to check out world news...to see what other countries' leaders are up to. After all, instant access to global news is the best thing about the internet.

Well, that, and midget clown porn.

We do this, this world-leader-watching, partly for reassurance that we're not the *only* country in the galaxy being run by clueless idiots, but also because *somebody's* got to keep an eye on these power junkies, these attention-gulping maniacs. I mean, anybody who has an actual *army* on their speed dial...

I know we've lost a lot of the serious freaks, some of the top-shelf psychos-with-a-government: Ming, Mao, Muammar Gaddafi, Papa Doc, Idi Amin, Boris & Natasha. But there are still some real droolers out there.

For example, there's Russian President Vladimir Putin, who used to be part of the Kremlin's infamous KGB until he was caught trying to smuggle in a second facial expression. Here's a man who prefers to be photographed half-naked, as if he were some kind of Cyrillic Miley Cyrus.

Another guy who's been in the news a lot lately (though he's usually clothed) is Malaysia's Prime Minister, Dato Sri Haji Mohammad Najib bin Tun Haji Abdul Razak, a man nobody's ever actually seen in public because his whole nizzle won't fit on those "Hi, my name is..." name tags. This is the guy who looks to be hands-down favorite for the next Nobel Prize in Advanced Incompetence, assuming John Boehner withdraws. PM Dato's national airline, you'll recall, lost an entire Boeing 777 and then insisted on searching in areas like Iceland, and New York's Finger Lakes, until Geraldo Rivera convinced him to expand the search radius to include Aruba.

(Ultimately, the jet did turn up. It was hiding behind Dato's name.)

Lurking a bit closer to home, let's not forget Rob "smoke 'em if you got 'em" Ford, Toronto's happy-footed Mayor and Hypertension poster child. Big Rob seems to think the way to solve Canada's recreational drug problem is for him to snort up everything above the 49th Parallel before any curious college kids get a chance. My, such altruism. What a giver, eh?

And an honorable mention surely must go to the President of Myanmar, Thein Sein, and his spouse, Khin Khin Win, for being the only heads of state we know whose names *both* rhyme. As far as we know, Sein's only crime so far wasn't technically a case of corruption; it was more of a bad PR judgment: he was photographed next to Hillary in a robin's-egg-blue pantsuit. (Her, not him.) Standing next to The Full Rodham wearing that outfit made the poor little guy look like a voodoo doll getting soul-kissed by a Macy's Parade Smurf balloon.

(By the way, Mr. Sein's full ceremonial title is "President of the Republic of the Union of Myanmar," which I think you'll agree is a much more manageable mouthful than trying to say "Burma.")

But for sheer over-the-top-ness, it's hard to touch those tiny tyrants from Pyongyang: the North Korean Kims.

Currently, North Koreans are enjoying the random whims marking the regime of Kim Jong-un, a fun era studded with benevolent blackouts, heady starvation, and random arrests. You've seen little Kim - the pudgy bantamweight with the wildly severe haircut, as if Edward Scissorhands got sent to reform school in Appalachia.

But those of you old enough to construct a sentence without shoving in the word "like" twelve times will also remember Kim Jong-un's daddy, Kim Jong-il.

At five-feet-two, Kim Jong-il was what psychiatrists would call "needy" -- what the rest of us would call "short." To compensate for being shorter than Granny Clampett's modeling career, Kim Jong-il used to insist on being called "Creator of the Universe" by the people of North Korea, who by then were too hungry to care ... they mostly just shuffled around muttering the Korean version of "dude, whatever."

Then, just to flesh out his status as a barking whackstick, he claimed to have invented the hamburger and was convinced Godzilla was a Communist.

And in a propaganda move unequaled before or since, North Korean school kids were taught that Kim Jong-il never defecated.

That would explain the grumpy look.

So, to be fair -- given the loose neckbolts on ol' Dad-- you'd have to admit that the next Kim, Kim Jong-un, came from a pretty scarred family tree trunk, sanity-wise. Even so, in any global Greatest Hits list of creative résumé padding, this latest Lil Kim is climbing the charts.

Witness:

- He is a computer wizard who's using a Xbox to plan nuclear war against the U.S. Hopefully, Matthew Broderick and Ally Sheedy will leap out of the movie *War Games*, beat Lil Kim to the gulch, and stop his evil plan. One thing we know for a fact: if we're waiting on Secretary of State John Kerry to do anything about anything, we'd be much better off conjuring up two imaginary teenage movie characters.
- The first time Kim ever picked up a set of golf clubs, he shot 11 holes-in-one. And that was just on the *front* nine.

- He is the uncle of a kid who flew to the Sun -- in one day -- and brought back samples. Of course, the kid's not an idiot: he made the trip at night.
- He fed his *own* uncle to a bunch of starving dogs. Actually, several "reliable" online sources are debunking this claim, but as you'd expect in Kim's case, even the denial is dingo-howl crazy. Not only did Kim Jong-un's PR people apparently make up the story about Kim feeding his uncle to wild dogs ... they made up the story because they thought it would enhance Kim's image. Enhance his image with *whom?* Michael Vick?
- For some time now, North Korean men have been forced to choose from 28 Kim-approved hairstyles. But according to a recent online article, Dear Leader has banned 27 of the possible dos. He's issued a directive mandating that all male Koreans get a haircut like his. As if freezing and starving wasn't bad enough.
- He discovered a burial site that archaeologists with Appalachian-truant haircuts insist is that of Dangun Wanggeom, founder of the first Korean kingdom. Dangun, the "grandson of heaven," was the son of a god and an unusually upwardly-mobile bear that turned into a woman. (*see 'Hillary Clinton'*)
- Kim's favorite house guest is Dennis Rodman.
- No, really.

And now, the wee berserker with the industrial-accident hairdo says he's found a unicorn.

Now, if such a claim had come from some psychotic cave troll, or Al Sharpton, we could just medicate the moonbat and move on. But this is Kim Jong-un; the first golfer in history to have a negative handicap. Let's show some respect.

As it turns out, there is in fact a creature nicknamed the Asian unicorn, but it has more than one horn (see *'Bill Clinton'*). This extremely rare animal is known locally as a *saola*, and until a late 2010 sighting in Laos, nobody had seen one for ten years. (*see 'Barack Obama's foreign policy'*)

On the bright side, caring environmentalist captured the saola, shoved it in a cage, and spirited the endangered multi-corn off to Bolikhamxay Provincial Agriculture College (*Home of the Fighting Bamboo!*) so all those caring environmentalists could study its ways. Unfortunately, one of its ways was being an uncaged animal, so it died.

But the story ends well. The ex-unicorn can now vote in Chicago.

Dark Days at Wiener World

Based on a true, and very stupid, story

<>~<>~~~~~~~~~~<>~<>~~~~~~~~~~<>~<>

Looking back on everything -- all the clues, all the mice, and what-all -- looking back, maybe the law here in my town of Creyer (it's pronounced "Cur") should've seen the connection. But even the F.B. of I. might not've corrugated the seemingly undulated links between some fool stealing a forklift, a ATM, *and* a snake.

I mean, something like this, it's like to stump ol' Sheriff Andy over by Mayberry.

Not to mention Barney.

Here's the particulates, as originally released by the Creyer Police. A couple days ago, according to Officer Scott "Scooter" Downe, a person or so broke in to Cotton Mather Elementary, ran down to the Cheerful Cherubs choir room, and stole a snake. Seems the little Cherubs were planning to enter the now-ripped-off reptile in this year's Everglades Python

Challenge down there in Davie, Florida, where a Baptist snake of that size might easily land them a $1,000 first prize.

As it turns out, the snake is something snake-types call a ball python, according to Curlene Getwilder, Otto and Candy Getwilder's troubled daughter. (Curlene's been staffing the info desk at the Creyer Saints of the Confederacy and Sanctified Serpentarium while her parents and a magistrate work out some pesky "personal recognizance" issues.)

A reporter from Creyer's weekly paper, *The Literable Gazette*, dashed over to Cotton Mather E., hoping to harvest some vital crime scene details. But he was unable to get anything quotable from the Cherubs' distraught choir director, Randy Leggins. Randy seemed unusually hysterical, even for a man wearing a Panama hat and a lime-green unitard who's in charge of children and just misplaced a mammal-eating serpent.

One night later, more bad news. Somehow, some bad seeds managed to steal a whole ATM right smack out of the parking lot down at Tyrell's Pole Dancing And Lunch Buffet.

The missing cash machine was reported to the CPD around 6am by Teencie Glock and several of the other matrons from Our Ladies of Perpetual Gastritis. The Ladies were just wrapping up an all-night vigil for the Cherubs' missing python, complete with blame chants and a sympathetic group clench, and Teencie needed a few dollars to treat the girls to some coffee and a breakfast biscuit over at the Sonic. But instead of a welcoming, well-lit ATM, all Teencie and the matrons saw was crumbled concrete and a skittering handful of extremely lost mice.

So many questions; so few answers. Creyer was waking up to an upside-down world.

And then come to find out that the ATM theft had been recilitated by the use of a hot-wired forklift.

According to Officer Downe, the suspects who'd asconded with the ATM had "liberated" an unattended forklift from down the street at Cecil's Trough & Lube, where it had been left overnight for an oil change. (It was a nice one, too, according to the Trough & Lube's owner/operator, Cecil Sawsill: a sweet Doosan GX series D30G, your standard counterbalanced Class IV packing a 3.3 liter Kubota diesel with a planetary drive axle. Those babies got a 24" load center and ODB brakes ... but you already knew that.)

The *Gazette's* reporter couldn't get a statement right away, on account of Cecil was out on a tow job. Just in front of Wiener World out by the four-lane, some hyper-caffeinated driver piloting a Rodents R Us delivery truck had misjudged and overturned, the truck's side panel got punctured by Wiener World's 8-foot model of a French's mustard, and out poured the truck's surprise payload: a river of tiny grey mice.

(A Wiener World regular said all those scurrying mice reminded her of that bedtime story about the Pie Biker of Hamblin. Cecil, ever the pragnotist, said it was too bad somebody stole that snake.)

Anyway, back at Tyrell's: Scooter figures the future forklift-lifting felons had maneuvered the forklift's forks under the

ATM's ... um ... Ms, levered the mast, worked the ATM into the bed of a pickup, and the rest was all getaways and grand larceny.

This was not good. At first it was just a furloined reptile. Now, somebody had nicked a cash machine and a forklift that was low on oil. Now, it qualified as a spree.

(At this point, the mice were still considered irreverent to the story.)

Creyer's Mayor, Carl "Big Carl" Sweeney, allowed that this was the worst crime wave he'd seen since the city bought one of those "smart" speed detectors (with the "YOUR SPEED IS..." digital readout and what-all) and some knucklehead stole the smart part. Big Carl let on that Creyer was getting a little too cosmopelican for raising children, including his own twin girls, Euphoria and Carl's Junior.

As you would expect, the usual suspects were rounded up, conterrogated, and (when their alamos checked out) reluctantly released:

- Tookey Ankle, night manager at Pawpaw's Fine Jewelry & Bait Shop, had been at work that night, uncrating a shipment of SpoorMaster cubic zirconium rebel super-teeny crappie square lips.
- Authorities couldn't question Dentitia "Eveready" Devereaux (the reigning queen from Creyer's Summer Solstice Double-Wide Parade And Guilt-Free Paternity Test), but didn't really need to: everybody knew she was somewhere out on the West Coast

filming outtakes for her reality show, *The Biggest Virginity Loser.*

- Tommy "Towhead" Grimes, owner of the "Grimes of Passion" adult boutique out by the landfill, had been up all night working on an ad for his annual Spring promotion, "Mother's Other Nature."
- Curlene Getwilder, or course, had an airtight excuse, since she was already *in* county lockup for that episode involving the Cuban boxer and the ferret.

So when the missing ATM turned up at the bottom of a quarried ravine *right behind Tyrell's place*, you could've knocked people over with a feather. (not Big Carl's twins, necessarily, but normal-sized people)

Later, during official questioning, Tyrell came clean. It was him who stole the python, figuring to work it into one of the pole dancer's acts. But the constrictor's appetite was also quickly consuming his life savings under there at Tyrell's Guestroom-Mattress Savings & Loan. So he struck upon the idea of busting into the ATM.

Which was when he called Rodents R Us and ordered a San Diego Zoo-sized load of mice, C.O.D.

Which he'd pay for from the ATM.

Which, when jimmied open, contained twelve bucks.

Which was why Tyrell quarry-launched the ATM.

Which, it turns out, was a nice model from ATMs R Us, your standard counterbalanced Class IV cash machine with a planetary drive axle.

Which, Tyrell learned a bit too late, he could've sold on the black market for $300,000.

"That Tyrell," Big Carl chuckled later that evening, as he gingerly navigated the mouse gauntlet at Wiener World. "He may not be smart, but he sure is stupid."

Flight Something-or-Other

Welcome to Malaise Air!

<>~<>~~~~~~~~~~<>~<>~~~~~~~~~~<>~<>

It's a puzzler that's barely a week old, and it's already become the biggest mystery in the history of flight.

No, not "Why is Security strip-searching Grandma?"

Not that mystery. The other one.

In terms of notoriety, the David Copperfield-like disappearance of Malaysia Airlines Flight 370 has eclipsed all earlier air travel enigmas -- all the previous unsolved posers, like

- What happened to Amelia Earhart?
- What *really* goes on in the Bermuda Triangle?
- How come a tuna fish sandwich that's three bucks at the deli costs $24 at the airport?
- Is that an *ashtray* in my armrest? Just how old *are* these seats?

- Why do airport security personnel always look like the 'before' pictures in a Nutri-System ad?
- Who is the company that makes those little foil bags that only hold three peanuts?

And not only has a whole plane vanished -- and *stayed* vanished -- but the staggeringly inept authorities in charge of *finding* the plane are bozos beyond belief. Half the time, they don't even get the plane's *flight number* right.

If anybody ever creates a Nobel Prize for numb-headed incompetence, these rubes are a lock.

Or maybe it's just me; I don't know. Here's the timeline. *You* decide.

Saturday, 8 March

- Malaysia Airlines Flight 370 takes off from Kuala Lumpur, despite the galley being desperately low on three-peanut foil bags.
- The flight's final destination is Beijing, assuming the pilots manage to spot a runway under the Chinese capital's world-class smog cloak.
- Shortly after takeoff, Malaysia Airlines announce that Flight 307 might possibly be missing, or not, maybe, though they're not sure, because nobody can find the key to the traffic control tower.
- Malaysian authorities announce that Flight 37 lost contact with air control at 2:21am, but then retract the claim after admitting they forgot to factor in Daylight Savings Time.

- Interpol issues an alert that two of the passengers on the missing flight are traveling on stolen European Union passports. The EU cannot be reached for comment, as they're all on the phone with their brokers in the Ukraine, dumping shares of Crimea Electric & Gas.
- Malaysian authorities issue an update, claiming that Flight 337 lost contact with air control at 1.21am, but then retract the claim after remembering they don't use Daylight Savings Time.
- Vietnamese officials say they've spotted an oil slick that could be from the missing plane. Officials in Beijing say they can't see a blasted thing in all this smog.
- Late in the day, a press conference is hastily wired up so reporters can get an update on Flight 007 from Malaysia's Prime Minister, Dato' Sri Haji Mohammad Najib bin Tun Haji Abdul Razak. Unfortunately, by the time all the reporters finish confirming how the PM's name is spelled, the update is out of date.

Sunday, 9 March

- Malaysian authorities express concerns about terrorism, especially now that it's getting dark an hour earlier.
- A spokesman from Malaysian Airlines claims to have proof that Flight 7003 may have turned back toward Kuala Lumpur, possibly to pick up some more peanuts.
- Vietnamese officials say they've spotted debris that could be from the

missing plane. The claim is retracted when the debris turns out to be a catering truck abandoned in '79 by the film crew of *Apocalypse Now*.

- The Malaysian Air Force admits their radar detected an unidentified object, but then retract the claim after the anomalous blip turns out to be Toronto Mayor Rob Ford.
- Conspiracy theorists tweet that the plane was abducted by aliens from a planet that treats peanuts as currency.

Monday, 10 March

- In the face of mounting international charges of incompetency, Malaysian authorities widen the search radius to 100 nautical miles, which would be great if they were searching Lake Erie.
- China expresses displeasure with Malaysia, threatening to drastically reduce the number of items on their take-out menu.
- Malaysia's Navy sends all both of its ships to investigate the alleged sighting of a life raft, but the Vietnamese get there first, commission the life raft, and start their *own* Navy. Congress immediately approves $650 billion in military aid for Vietnam freedom fighters, assuming there are any.
- Conspiracy theorists tweet that the plane was abducted in Aruba by Joran van der Sloot.
- Malaysian authorities widen the search area to include India, Indonesia, and Mordor.

Wednesday, 12 March

- In a Wall Street Journal article, US investigators claim the missing Boeing 777 kept flying for several hours after it vanished, as if the plane were some kind of stingy peanut-dispensing zombie.
- Vietnamese officials say they've spotted debris that could be the missing plane's tail. Malaysian officials tell Vietnam to please shut up already. Vietnam responds by threatening to unleash the full force of their naval armada, just as soon as they finish camouflaging the raft.
- Interpol now says the two guys with stolen passports are not terrorists, but are probably illegal immigrants. When President Obama hears this news, he responds by giving the two guys free health care, granting them in-state tuition to the University of Chicago, and appointing one of the guys ambassador to Greenland.
- Conspiracy theorists tweet that the plane malfunctioned due to global warming, causing Al Gore to grow another jowl.

Friday, 14 March

- Malaysian authorities expand the search area to include the entire Indian Ocean, Ireland, and East St. Louis.
- India gets involved in the search, dispatching three ships, three aircraft, and 200 million telemarketers.
- Desperate Malaysia Airlines execs call in Basil Rathbone, The Amazing Kreskin, Herve Villechaize, and Dog the Bounty Hunter.
- Interpol now says the two guys with stolen passports are Chinese nationals posing as Malaysians in order to

get a shot on *Southeast Asia's Got Talent!* When the A&E network hears this news, they offer the two guys a six-season deal for a reality TV series called *Peking Duck Dynasty*.

- Conspiracy theorists tweet that Malaysian officials keep getting Flight 730's flight number wrong. The conspiracy theorists add up all the wrong numbers, triangulate locations, and conclude that the missing flight landed at a biker bar in Daytona Beach.

Saturday 15 March

- An alert reporter notes that the Malaysian government has now retracted more claims than they made in the first place.
- Search teams from India are unable to locate the missing plane; however, they do convince several Malaysians to switch to Verizon.
- Malaysian authorities expand the search area to include the Crab Nebula, Disney's *Pirates of the Caribbean* ride, and the 18th Century.
- Conspiracy theorists tweet that today is the Ides of March, and then they nod knowingly, which is not easy to do in a tweet.
- At this point, a rogue gang of reality theorists who'd heard just about enough of this conspiracy nonsense geolocated the conspiracy theorists and gang-slapped them into silence. (*see 'Nobel Prize'*)

See what I mean? These guys couldn't find an M in a bag of M&Ms.

Oh, yeah. Before I go, here's a late-breaking update. According to satellite data released by the Vietnamese Navy and America's ambassador to Greenland, Malaysian authorities are now confirming that Flight 333 was definitely headed either north or south.

Probably.

Pain by Numbers

Hmm. Looks like a 10.T67.455ZD. Now, cough.

<>~<>~~~~~~~~~~<>~<>~~~~~~~~~~<>~<>

Oh, good. ObamaCare just got picky.

This is a new twist. Until now, the "Affordable" Health Care Act has just been unaffordable, indecipherable, inconsistent, impersonal, unsecured, down for repairs, and short on doctors. And hospitals. And health care.

Now it's neurotic, too.

America, please say 'hello' to the ICD-10.

As every American schoolchild knows, unless they've been suspended for waving an American flag on Cinco de Mayo, the ICD is one of many acronyms used by the WHO acronym at the UN acronym. The UN is an international anachronism, a collection of professionally impotent people from many countries whose sole qualification, apparently, is owning a funny hat. Members of the UN meet regularly in New York City to dine on an expense account and not pay parking tickets.

WHO is or are the public health arm or arms of the UN, and the WHO charter looks simple enough: to churn out endless PR commercials for WHO. When they're not busy making promos, they're busy making sure everybody on Earth has access to birth control, and the occasional book. But no candy.

And that brings us to the ICD, and it's latest ObamaCare incarnation, the ICD-10. The International Classification of Diseases (ICD) is a codified system for classifying medical symptoms, diagnoses, and treatments ... and - most importantly to ObamaCare - for denying payments. It is a superfast, increasingly digital way for doctors to share information quickly between insurance companies, ungoverned government agencies, and Chinese computer hackers.

Basically, before ObamaCare, the procedure worked like this:

- Old Uncle Lars keeps complaining about his "dadburn gut"
- You point out that, for over three decades, Uncle Lars has eaten nothing but fried fish sticks
- Finally you take Uncle Lars to the doctors
- The doctors quickly figure out that old Lars has an ulcer
- But the doctors run a $68,000 battery of tests anyway so nobody gets sued
- The doctors look up 'ulcer' and see it doesn't really pay much, so...

- Using the ICD, the doctors decide on a better diagnosis for Lars and recommend a intrathoracic esophagoesophagostomy (ICD-9-CM 42.51)
- Your insurance company notifies you that having an Uncle is a pre-existing condition
- After a thoughtful family discussion, the family decides to shove old Uncle Lars out to sea on a slab of ice
- The family achieves closure by gathering to watch an all-new *American Idol*

And, basically, since ObamaCare, the song remains the same. But now the ICD is evolving.

When a French physician originally came up with the Bertillon Classification of Causes of Death in 1893, there were just 44 items on the list, items like:

- Ulcer, General
- Ulcer, Fish Stick Induced
- Ennui
- Guillotine Proximity Disorder
- Complications due to way too much butter
- Falling down on a pointy stick
- Horse injuries, General (dismount, kicked by, thrown from)
- Horse injuries, Specialized (Catherine the Great)
- Forgetting to run away

After the first revision, five years later, the list had grown to 161 codes. By the sixth revamp in 1948, the thing needed two volumes.

And then the US Federal Government got involved.

ICD-10's predecessor (cleverly named ICD-9) contained some 17,000 codes. Suddenly, now that the government was involved, your second toe needed a different diagnostic code than your big toe, or your middle toe, and different codes for the other foot, too.

But now, we've upped the ante. Now, those crack medical professionals at the IRS are in charge of your health care.

The new ICD-10? One hundred fifty-five thousand codes.

In just over 120 years, we've come up with 3,500 times as many ways to call in sick.

Like the numb, nutty IRS itself, the all-new IRS-driven ICD-10 codes range from the mundane (Pain in right forearm, billable) to the sublime (Removal of Autologous Tissue Substitute from Thoracic Duct, Percutaneous Approach); from the obvious (Heartburn) to the obscure (Suicide by jellyfish) to the downright ignorant (Suicide by jellyfish, subsequent encounter).

Here are some more actual items on the list to ponder:

- Self-inflicted drowning (you know, if the jellyfish thing doesn't work out)

- Latent wet crab yaws (I don't know what this is, but if you have it, please call *before* you drop by)
- Acquired night blindness (Also known as "standing outside in the dark like an idiot." It's curable. Even with guys.)
- Exposure to abnormal gravitational forces (I don't know if this refers to the effects of a black hole, or the effects of a buffet)
- Contact with a duck (has this become a problem?)
- Radiculitis (it's really not as radiculous as it sounds)
- Certain zoonotic bacterial diseases (*zoonotic* is, I think, similar to *hypnotic*, but with more elephants)
- There's a code for getting bitten by a sea lion -- but no code for getting bitten by a regular lion. (There's also a code for "other contact with sea lion." I don't even want to know.)
- There's also a separate code in case you get struck by a shark. Not bitten, mind you; *struck*. (maybe the shark has Acquired Night Blindness)
- Injuries sustained from playing drums (There are separate codes for piano, string, and wind & brass. Of course.)
- Ichthyoparasitism due to Vandellia cirrhosa (as opposed to ichthyoparasitism due to exposure to the drummer from Martha and the Vandellas)
- Spacecraft collision (unless caused by abnormal gravitational forces)
- Forced landing of spacecraft, injuring occupant (I'm guess that if somebody forces you to land your spaceship, filing with Blue Cross is probably *not* your most pressing issue)

- Contact with nail gun, subsequent encounter (What do you do? You've *already* said "*ow*" and you obviously don't know what "*Duck!*" means.)

So let's get moving, America! Get out there and hurt yourself! You're covered!

Mostly.

IRS Warning: Should you get struck by a latent blind orchestra conductor with crab yaws, you're on your own.

If you get struck a *subsequent* time, be sure to wave at Uncle Lars.

Bread, Milk and Bombogenesis

Life in the Two-Feet-Deep South

<>~<>~~~~~~~~~~<>~<>~~~~~~~~~~<>~<>

Last week, here in South Carolina, it snowed again. That's twice now this decade.

This is getting out of hand.

And all across the arctically-afflicted areas, we reacted according to the time-honored script:

- Buy bread & milk
- Race to the ATM and get some cash (in case we lose power and have to buy bread & milk from the trunk of some guy's car)
- Close the schools (which is stupid because they're *loaded* with bread & milk)
- Drive too fast and rear-end a car...in the neighbor's yard

See, snow is Mother Nature's way of protecting stores that sell white bread. And, of course, milk. If Southerners lived in the Snow Belt, we'd have the strongest bones on in the galaxy.

When it was all over (in other words, the next day), it was estimated that some 32 million loaves of bread had been purchased. To put that into perspective, if Barack Obama promised every person in America 32 million dollars, I wouldn't be a bit surprised.

Even more bizarre was the storm's timing. Here we were in the American South, preparing for 6-12 inches of global warming; meanwhile, in Russia, it was a comrade-chilling *61 degrees* at the Winter Olympics, which for some reason were being held in a construction site at a Black Sea beach resort that's infested with wild dogs.

Here in the South, we get a lot of grief for our "over-reaction" to winter weather, but we're just not tactically prepared for it; we just don't have the tools, the skills and, except for New Orleans, the political graft to deal with it.

I'm not sure why our up-map relatives mock our reactions to winter. It's not like we sit around laughing at them every time they finish a book, or get sideswiped by a moose, or move to Florida and wear plaid shorts.

Heat, we understand. Cold, not so much. South Carolina is a place where in August we get what's known as theoretical humidity - because sometimes the humidity actually climbs *over* 100% and theoretically it can't do that. Quantum humidity.

Forget snowmen. Sometimes our *roads* melt.

(Personally, I'm snowman-challenged. I couldn't do it. I've never bought a carrot in my life.)

On the other hand -- given the rarity of winter precipitation, and our gentle, easy-going temperament, we Southerners *appreciate* the snow more than most.

For about one day.

Then the muttering begins...followed by the daredevil driving. This week in South Carolina, highway patrol logged over 4,500 incidents, including nearly fifteen hundred traffic accidents and an unconfirmed sighting of a driver allegedly using a turn signal.

Residents were repeatedly (and futilely) offered two words of advice: "Stay home" -- which more often than not morphs into "Watch this."

This last storm hit us in waves. The initial recon unit was nice and friendly: great huge flakes dropping from a muted sky. But the infantry was all business. Anger and attitude. Icy little bits rifling by in 15-25 mph winds. Testy.

If snow storms were women, this is the one I'd end up dating.

Snow-zilla's ripple effect was unusually widespread. Due to wicked weather in Atlanta, some 9,000 flights nationally were cancelled. On the bright side, many flights were diverted to Chicago, though the checked bags went to Dallas. Fortunately, baggage became a moot point when the passengers re-routed to Chicago were all gunned down by street gangs and other local politicians.

(Eventually, the storm stomped its way up the I-95 corridor, killing 8 million people who live in Amtrak.)

Of course, the local weather people live for this stuff. Not only do they get to interrupt normal network fare, like *CSI: Metrosexuals* and reruns of *Buffy Impacts a Molar*, it also gives them a chance to trot out their scientific-yet-caring weather graphics, like Your Five-At-Six Exclusive Hi-Def Live Mega-Doppler Pan-Galactic Weather Radar.

The problem with Your Five-At-Six Exclusive Hi-Def Live Mega-Doppler Pan-Galactic Weather Radar is that by the time my Your Five-At-Six Weather Dude finishes pronouncing it, the weather has changed.

To be sure, we appreciate the updates on closings; delays; the Pan-Galactic Radar explanations (in TV Weatherland, it seems, rain is green, snow is blue, and ice is pink). It's important that their viewing audience knows it's snowing (in case somebody doesn't own a window, or has some kind of rare pink-blue colorblindness).

But after alerting us that it was snowing, they were pretty much out of ideas. At one point, our Local Weather Person shared this: "Clearly, we've stepped outside."

Whew. That is some bold meteorological analysis.

Granted, some closings were more dire than others. A business called Skyland Nephrology was shuttered, leaving who knows how many nephs unchecked.

Even more frightening was the "not today" news from the Saber County Academy of Advanced Cosmetology. Imagine *that* company's clientele running around in public, without even the efforts of future beauticians.

It's not for the faint-hearted.

Government disaster agencies also kept us updated (yes, 'government disaster' *is* redundant, but now's not the time for a civics lesson). They made sure we knew two things:

- They're on top of the situation
- They need more money

Mid-blizzard, South Carolina's governor placed the entire state under a Civil Emergency. Now *that's* serious. Last time that happened, Hooters had run out of hot wings.

But the storm subsided quickly, almost as quickly as it had begun. Crazy stuff. Two weeks ago, an ice storm...this week, half a foot of snow and sleet.

What next, an earthquake?

Yeah, right.

Why Children Shouldn't Run with Caesars

Julius, we hardly knew ye

One of my resolutions for this new year's orbit was to read more books. That, and marry a furiously rich blind woman who lives on a different continent.

I did find some books.

It was a realization that kind of crept up on me, but I've discovered that, in my ongoing war to write a humor column every week, one of the bloodied casualties has been unfettered time to *read.* Of course, I'm sure many other staggeringly successful money-raking artistes struggle with such problems. Paula Deen, after cooking on TV all day long, probably doesn't eat much.

Okay, bad example.

Anyway, this year I've been reading the latest in the "*Killing...*" series from *The O'Reilly Factor*'s Bill O'Reilly -- you know the batch: *Killing Lincoln; Killing Kennedy; Killing the Bad Witch; Killing the Other Bad Witch; Killing Random People Named Andy; Killing Nick Nolte's Career; Killing a Perfectly Good Weekend;* and so on.

Let's pray the man never develops an interest in maiming.

They're all very enjoyable books, especially the ones that exist. And so I was looking forward to the series' most recent edition, *Killing Jesus*, which is about Jesus of Nazareth.

Eventually.

See, within the covers of *Killing Jesus*, for motivations that may never be explained to us little people, the author only managed to stay on-topic for some 22 brief pages before veering wildly off into what was apparently an entirely different book: *Killing Julius*, maybe, or *Those Whacky Caesars!*

Don't get me wrong - O'Reilly's the author; he can follow his own muse. If a person wants to title their book *How To Grow Borscht On a Budget* and then inexplicably carom off into a disjointed discussion about Appalachian cabinet hinges, that's their business. But it makes things tough for the audience to keep up - that's all I'm saying. It would be like Al Sharpton talking about Peyton Manning and then suddenly blaming blizzards in Atlanta on racism.

Okay, bad example.

For whatever reason, however, the author of *Killing Jesus* felt that before he plowed into his professed topic, his readers first needed to know a whole lot about something else: namely, that

Julius Caesar and his posse were possibly the most dysfunctional family since Henry Tudor invented the wife buffet.

As every schoolchild who's not busy texting knows, Gaius Julius Caesar was a famous Roman general who, around the year 50 B.C., invented his own calendar because he was tired of everybody in B.C. having to count the years backwards. When he was fifty-five years old, this Caesar was stabbed to death by the Senate, which could never happen today because it would require consensus.

On the day of his death (March the Ides), Julius had been forewarned at least twice that something bad was about to happen, once by Calpurnia, his third wife (*see 'forewarned at least twice'*). After waking from a horrible nightmare, Calpurnia had pleaded with her husband not to go to the office, begging him to just proclaimo in sick. Additionally, a psychic named Spurinna had predicted dire events on this day, based on the hard science of staring at the raw livers of sacrificed chickens, in much the same way that network TV executives come up with new sitcoms today.

But no. Stubborn, haughty Julius just scoffed, told his wife "Hey, frigidus out" -- and the reliquum is historia.

Later that day, around Ides-thirty, Caesar's salad was tossed by some sixty dagger-sporting men in robes with monogram-challenging monikers like Decimus Junius Brutus Albinus, Publius Servilius Casca Longus, and Tonius Sopranus. The finishing blow was delivered by Brutus, who got Jules right in the obscenum, causing the not-so-divine-after-all emperor to shout, in an unnaturally high-pitched voice, "Et tu, Brute?" (literal translation: *for real, dog?*)

Despite having declared himself immortal, Caesar than did what most people do after being stabbed about eleven hundred times by cross-dressing Congressmen: he died, making him eligible to vote in Chicago. Year's later, his immortality was assured, when somebody named an OB-GYN procedure after him.

But that was just the *final* chapter, for *that* Caesar. Just a...

...Caesarean section.

<groanius>

In Egypt, either IV years earlier or later (there's that confounded B.C. thing again), XXI-year-old Cleopatra and her XIII-year-old brother, Ptolemy, are busily playing a friendly game of Who Kills Who First. But they can't really stay focused because Julius suddenly sails into Alexandria, hot on the trail of the fleeing Pompey, a spinach-eating sailor who's forever fighting with Brutus over olive oyl rites.

(Brutus, by the way, was not just one of Julius' murderers - he was probably Caesar's illegitimate son from yet another affair, this one with a friend's wife, Servilia Caepionis. *And now, folks, a brief word from our sponsor, Pagan Adriatic Cruises! Next vacation, go Pagan -- dining, decadence, debauchery, shuffleboard -- and leave the driving to us!*)

Pompey has managed, somehow, to simultaneously be Julius' brother-in-law *and* his son-in-law, so taking out Pompey would qualify Julius for a twofer, giving Caesar a mid-season ERA (Earned Roman Assassination) of 3.01 -- not bad for a man in his mid-Ls.

Suddenly, just after the commercial break, Pompey is beheaded by Ptolemy's conniving eunuch, Potheinos, though we're thinking that if this Potheinos dude had really been all *that* conniving, he wouldn't have let himself get, you know, eunuched.

(For the record, Ptolemy's ancestor, Ptolemy, killed his own mother, who had killed her own husband, who was having an affair with her own mother. These people were like a living country-and-western song, with pyramids.)

Upon hearing that somebody else had killed Pompey first, Julius was so heartbroken that he had sex with Cleopatra.

Historical Note: as part of his Cleo-centered recuperative therapy, Big J the C also continued to sleep with his wife, his mistresses, and pretty much anything else that moved in the northern hemisphere, including a king named Nicomedes in northern Turkey -- a broad palette of self-medication from which we get the famous Latin quotation, *Quae est patris tui?* ("Who's your daddy?")

Until then, Julius had fathered only one legitimate child - his daughter Julia, who had married...you guessed it...Pompey, the formerly full-headed statesman. But now, Cleo gives birth to a son, and with a straight face names him Philopator Philometor

Caesar, virtually guaranteeing the kid will never get a prom date.

Naturally, Julius invites Cleo and Phil Phil back to Rome -- *to live in the same house with Calpurnia.* And at this point, we shouldn't be a bit surprised. I mean, Julius may be an immortal, but he's still a *guy* immortal.

The spurned Calpurnia slips into a depressed funk and spends her days scarfing pints of Haagen-Dazs gelato. Next, the addled emperor even manages to snub Cleo, when he adopts his nephew Octavian and names *him* heir to the empire.

And then, of course, came the Ides. Julius went to the Senate and got his circulatory system vetoed.

Finally, just before the top of the hour, everybody left alive in the story went to war. Brutus & Cassius bought an army at Legions 'R' Us, using a post-dated check, which was a brilliant move given that backwards-counting B.C. calendar. Octavian teamed up with Marc Antony, a gallant general with an impressive list of résumé bullets:

- raging alcoholism
- muscular legs
- American Idol finalist
- pedophilia
- has slept with Cleopatra *and* Jennifer Lopez

Over the next dozen years, the rest of the cast mostly just killed themselves, unwittingly providing fodder for several more Bill O'Reilly books. First Cassius, then Brutus, then

Marc, then Cleo. Finally, just to be a contrarian, Octavian deep-sixed Phil Phil and then, as befits an august Caesar, he gave himself a new name:

Barack Obama.

Okay, bad example.

My Worst Job Ever

Yet.

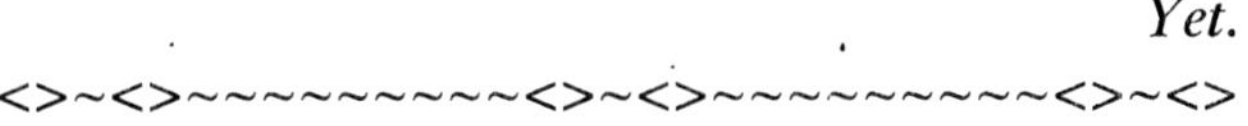

Once upon a time, I had a job, and my boss was a bipolar dwarf.

It didn't really work out.

We called the dwarf Turbeaux -- not to his face, of course. We called him Turbeaux about a foot *above* his face.

Because, you know, he's a dwarf.

Turbeaux was a vile little creature with a Montana-sized temper and a Barbados-sized fuse. I'd taken a job as a website developer for an ad agency, and Turbeaux had somehow managed to get himself hired as head of the department, apparently because he'd wowed management with some more-or-less memorized internet buzz words, like *hits*, and *google it*, and *porn*.

In many ways, Turbeaux was a gift. At any moment, he'd spew some deliciously ignorant malaprop:

- We need to register both of those ptomaines
- Let's focus on surge engine optimization
- Okay, stroll down. Keep strolling.

Fanning the flame was the fact that this doomed, short-lived stint with the bipolar dwarf was my first gig in eight years working for someone else, if you don't count the IRS. It also represented the first time -- after eight calm, productive, sanity-filled years working from home -- that I would not only have to go to somebody's offices, but I'd have to stay there all day, all week, every week.

So. If you start with those handicaps and then throw in a bipolar dwarf with bad 'tude and a serious case of Short Man Syndrome...well, it didn't really work out.

But no matter how bad things are, things could always be worse. I can imagine a lot of jobs that, for various reasons, would be way worse than just hanging around waiting for the veins to pop in a bipolar dwarf's forehead.

For example, one of *these* could be your worst job ever, because...

...because of the people you'd have to work for

- Security expert at Target
- Morals coach for the US Congress
- Nick Nolte's barber

- John Boehner's joke writer
- The RN saddled with colonoscopy prep for Toronto Mayor Rob Ford
- The kid who delivers the paper to Kim Jong Un
- Ozzy Osbourne's official interpreter for trips to the Vatican
- Staff in charge of White House blame-shifting
- Vladimir Putin's food taster
- Rob Ford's food taster
- Whoever ghost-writes Geraldo Rivera's autobiography
- The guy who provides the "global situation" daily debrief to Joe Biden
- Miley Cyrus' therapist
- Miley Cyrus' therapist's therapist

...because of the people you'd have to work with

- Sensitivity trainer for the Seattle Seahawks
- Security system salesman in Appalachia
- Birthday party rent-a-clown in Stephen King's hometown
- Manager of a kosher deli in South Georgia
- Voice coach for Roseanne Barr's "National Anthem" comeback
- Bathroom attendant at the Malibu Barbie Bulimia Institute
- Any *Factor* guest who doesn't agree with Bill O'Reilly
- Burqa saleswoman who got stuck with the *Victoria's Secret* route

- Owner of a Buick dealership in that part of Pennsylvania where people call each other "thee"
- Bartender at the Cotton Mather Youth Summer Camp
- Cast extra for the Quentin Tarantino remake, *Snow White & the Seven Meth-Addicted Dwarves*
- Baskin-Robbins franchisee in Fargo
- Confession priest at the NSA
- The cheerleading coach at Kabul Junior High
- Hot tub maintenance at Big Lucy's Dude Ranch for the Morbidly Obese

...because of the things you'd have to do

- Dennis Rodman's dentist
- Paula Deen's foot massager
- Customer service rep at facebook's complaint center
- Gay Rights promoter in Daytona Beach during Bike Week
- Pizza delivery guy in Detroit
- The person responsible for updating the ObamaCare documentation
- Mount Rushmore orifice cleaner
- *The Wizard of Oz* stage manager in charge of winged monkeys
- Walmart greeter in Denver on Discount Marijuana Day
- Bicycle courier in Machu Picchu
- Medical examiner at Six Flags Over Chernobyl
- Justin Bieber's publicist-slash-bail bondsman
- A Jehovah's Witness in Haight-Ashbury

- The staffer who has to pick up Andrew Weiner's snaps at the PhotoMart
- Richard Simmons' personal valet
- Vegas airport security guard in charge of pat-downs during a Plus-Sized Model convention
- Hillary's fact checker

...because of the things you* couldn't *do

- Hillary's fact checker

~-~-~-~-~-~-~-~-~-~-~

See what I mean? And you thought *your* job was lame?

So. Next Monday morning, be thankful -- remember, no matter how bad things are, at least your job doesn't involve disposable gloves, Toronto's Mayor in a toss-away paper gown, and you saying:

"Okay, now cough."

Zakryt Rot - Eto Moya Ulybka

translation: "Shut up - that IS my smile."

<>~<>~~~~~~~~~~<>~<>~~~~~~~~~~<>~<>

It's almost over. Sometime tomorrow, the XXII Olympic Winter Games will officially end. And, as usual, NBC will provide live coverage.

About twelve hours later.

Yeah, I know. "Live coverage." Shh. Nudge, nudge; wink, wink.

But the XXII Games, since day I, have been a little odd.

The Games' opening ceremonies from Sochi, Russia, were a bit, well, glitchy. But at least the *closing* ceremonies look promising. Across the globe, millions of enrapt fans will be glued to their screens to see if Vladimir Putin displays his *other* facial expression.

Of course, we have to have Winter Olympics: otherwise, Americans would never get to see athletes with exotic-sounding names like Björgenslip Prudenprömbundkaller and Teurgenische Flörgenberchtesköllen. In a close finish, these guys could just stick out their name and win.

(By the way, how do you pronounce that weird o? You know, the ö sitting under the fang marks?)

Överall, 2014's Winter Games were okay, I suppose, as pan-national sporting events go, particularly pan-national sporting events that are winter weather-dependent, so that the host country decides to hold them at ... a beach resort.

And who came up with these sports? In one event, women belly-flop onto a travel-sized ironing board, head-first, and then blaze down an ice chute at 80+ miles an hour. The goal, I assume, being to out-shriek the other contestants. And to not die.

As it turns out, this Darwin Award-qualifying activity is known as the "skeleton." It's related to the "luge" except, in the luge, the ~~victims~~ contestants try not to die feet-first.

(According to the internet, "luge" means "a way to thin the herd of morons" whereas "skeleton" translates as "not enough morons were dying on the luge.")

I'm still trying to get my head around the biathlon - where armed guys in spandex ski uphill for a while, then stop and shoot stuff, then ski uphill again, then shoot at some more stuff, all at a brisk two miles an hour.

I guess this would come in handy if you were an exotic dancer working above the Arctic Circle and your village got invaded by the Marx Brothers.

And, of course, x-treme snowboarding has finally wormed its way into the Olympics. Snowboarding: that sultry siren singing to the face-pierced generation. Featuring events like the Cross, the Slopestyle, and the freestyle freebase half-crack pipe. Where the tactical plan is to "throw down" before you "chill out" and the pinnacle of success is "shredding it." Sponsored by Nestle's Tollhouse Cookies and the City of Denver.

So, as NBC unpacked their gear in Sochi, some Olympic-level oddness was to be expected.

Ill-fated, maybe. Pre-doomed. There certainly were plenty of clues, from the outset, that these particular Games might be beset by bummers:

- During the opening ceremony pyrotechnics, one of the five Olympic rings failed to light up. Next morning, by an odd coincidence, the opening ceremony pyrotechnicians failed to wake up.
- Regional terrorists had threatened to disrupt the Games by commandeering the local restaurants and serving nothing but beet soup.
- To anchor its entire Olympics coverage, NBC inexplicably chose a guy with a contagious face.
- Hotel guests were not impressed that the tap water was the same color as the Olympic medals.

- Several of the new snowboarding events had to be postponed so the athletes could complete puberty.
- Sochi temperatures whipsawed endlessly between the teens and the sixties, prompting hundreds of Russian Jews to migrate to South Florida.
- At one point, the terrorists kidnapped NBC co-desk jockey Matt Lauer. The next day they brought him back. NBC refused to accept the package. The kidnappers offered $4 million.
- Two words: tandem toilets

To acquire TV coverage rights, NBC had paid the International Olympic Committee the staggering sum of $775 million, nearly as much as they'd forked over to buy Brian Williams from Madame Tussauds.

But then, after dropping 775 large for the Olympics, *they forgot to actually show any Olympics.*

Who knows why...maybe Bob "Attack of the Red Raccoon" Costas had memorized all the camera cuts and then burned them in a snit after NBC yanked him and his punch line-spawning face off the set. Poor Bob. If his eyesight got any worse, he could referee college football in the Southeastern Conference.

Timing was certainly part of the problem. Depending on where you were in the US when you turned on your TV, the day's events in Sochi had already ended some nine to twelve hours earlier. (We're not counting Hawaii, where people are too high to care about the Olympics ... they're so laid-back they make Brian Williams look like Sam Kinison on a Snickers binge. Nor do we need to bother our Alaskan friends with any snow-based sports: in Alaska, it's not called a slalom; it's called a commute.)

And NBC kept trying to drag *us* into their time warp, too. At some point every night during the evening news, adult Americans would hear this from adult broadcasters at NBC:

"Okay, now we're going to show you who won medals today, so if you don't want to know, leave the room for a minute."

They were worried ... stay with me here ... they were worried that we would be disappointed if we got advance notice of old scores from future reruns recapping scores from events that had already happened last night.

But we can't lay it *all* on time zones and large quarantined heads. NBC simply chose to not show the Olympics during the Olympics. Instead, we got disjointed history and tepid tourism, like taped segments of some NBC reporter wearing Buddy Holly's glasses, running around the food courts of Sochi panhandling for free samples.

At one point during their 2014 Winter Games reportage, NBC actually aired an extended, studio-produced segment on the USA/USSR space race. Sadly, though, Putin's agents insisted on editing the moon landing bits for their home audience, so we all watched as a grainy Neil Armstrong planted a US flag ... in rural Arizona.

And then came a seemingly endless series of Tonya Harding/Nancy Kerrigan retrospectives.

Seriously, NBC? Still sopping the sauce of that scoop, are you? Got anything on Ireland's mid-1800's spud outage? How about Gutenberg and that exciting new 'book' idea?

I know I'm treating NBC like they're idiots, but that's only because they're idiots. Let's look at some lowlights:

~-~-~-~-~-~-~-~-~-~

NBC: "This is not the same team that competed in the 1988 Olympics."

Well, thank you, Captain Obvious.

~-~-~-~-~

NBC: "The best strategy is to get out in front."

Whew. These guys don't make enough money.

~-~-~-~-~

NBC: "She doesn't want to have to pass between two Koreans. The space is just too tight."

There's a slight in that comment, somewhere.

~-~-~-~-~

NBC's, like, Guest Snowboarding Expert: "It was awesome. She totally shredded it, but it was, like, a lot of scrutinization from the judges."

You know, as a world power, we may be 30th in Math; we may be 23rd in Science; but America leads the world in Dude.

~-~-~-~-~-~

NBC: "Maybe it wasn't quite the ending you were hoping for - you came in 64th - but..."

But, who knows? Four long, interminable years from now, maybe, if you stay focused, there's...nah. You're a glue stick.

~-~-~-~-~-~-~-~-~-~-~

So, stand tall, Team America. Like, totally throw down some shredding on your, like, scrutinization and stuff. Be sure to give our best to "Harpo" Putin, that zany, madcap laugh riot.

Bundle up and stay warm, too! We know you're competing in *terra incognita.* After all, when you suit up for cross-country skiing and half the contestants are wearing t-shirts, you know you're facing some stiff competition.

(Either that, or your flight got lost and you're suddenly in the Dollywood Olympics.)

And make us proud! We'll all be watching the previews of the reruns of yesterday's taped live Winter Games.

Except for curling. Curling, I wouldn't wish on anybody.

Not even Brian Williams.

The Gnaw Christie Minstrels

Some people are guilty until proven guilty.

<>~<>~~~~~~~~~~<>~<>~~~~~~~~~~<>~<>

This just in: according to an unnamed source, New Jersey's chronically evil Governor has unleashed a global-killing virus, sacked Rome, and eaten a raw goat.

Ladies and gentlemen, meet Chris Christie - America's current political piñata.

By now, you don't need me to recount the gory details of "Bridge-gate," the cruel, vile, heartless scandal that's shadowing Jersey's chief executive like Oprah tracking a donut...the story's gotten more coverage than the '69 moon landing. But the scope of this Traffic Cone outrage is off the charts. The media have lockjawed on the embattled Governor like a politician spotting a microphone.

It's been some time since we've seen the news media so determinedly focused on the total destruction of a public figure (can you say "Dubya?"). To call this rabid feeding frenzy "piling on" would be like saying Hitler "piled on" Poland. Compared to the Christie coverage, Charles Manson was just a keen Beatles fan.

And it's not as if there's been a shortage of nutbags in the news, either. Oh, no. The year 2014 has kicked off as an absolute carnival of crazy.

So let's play a game we often play round here. Below is a list of current events -- some are real news items plucked from today's headlines, some are bogus.

Your job is...well, you know what to do.

~-~-~-~-~-~-~-~-~-~

Today, a Navy F-18 jet crashed off the coast of Virginia. Just yesterday, in the same dangerous off-shore waters, the Coast Guard had to rescue civilians from a foundering sailboat. Al Gore blamed both events on global warming, so the ward nurse dialed up his Thorazine.

The White House responded to the news by signing an Executive Order mandating Republicans hold their 2016 National Convention off the coast of Virginia.

~-~-~-~-~-~

NBC News has uncovered more damaging information about Chris Christie. Not only did the increasingly tainted New Jersey Governor return a two-day-overdue library book in 1972, but once, at a family cookout, he served red wine with chicken.

~-~-~-~-~-~

Today, the Ninth Circuit Court of Appeals ruled that Coloradans can use food stamps to buy marijuana for recreational use. An impromtu celebration broke out in Aspen, in part due to a previously unread ObamaCare provision that allows ski boots and schnapps to be classified as "medical equipment."

~-~-~-~-~-~

CBS News is reporting that Governor Chris Christie has been sighted wearing white slacks after Labor Day.

Later tonight on *60 Minutes*, Sorely Wafer, Bread Adley, and the perky Katie Couric follow up on a stunning new accusation: allegedly, at a YMCA in 1968, the Jersey Governor didn't shower before using the pool.

~-~-~-~-~-~

In an effort to protect surfers from rising shark populations, officials in Western Australia have instituted a temporary cash bounty for hunters who shoot sharks.

This is in stark contrast to the approach taken by the American government, where whimpering "Save the Shark" lobbyists have won the right to shoot surfers instead.

~-~-~-~-~-~

ABC News, having broken the career-crippling story about Chris Christie re-gifting a holiday fruitcake, now reluctantly reports that, in the late 80s, the Governor may have returned a video tape to Blockbuster without rewinding it.

~-~-~-~-~-~

A popular weight loss program is claiming that, thank to their system, Americans have collectively lost millions of pounds; so many pounds, in fact, that Georgia Congressman Hank Johnson is afraid the United States might tip over.

~-~-~-~-~-~

"Hi. This is Nahkov Birkenstock, one of the many monotonic, irretrievably liberal DJs here at NPR. We interrupt our fascinating exposé about housecat obesity to bring you the emotionally-charged news that New Jersey Governor Chris Christie has been hauled in for questioning after allegations that he once split an infinitive.

"It's just the latest in a damning, Dorian Gray-like cascade of failures by the Garden State's leader, this fallen Adam who just last week, you'll remember, finally admitted to tearing that 'Do Not Remove' tag off a mattress.

"And now, back to our fund-raising telethon, which has been going on non-stop since, oh, about 1948."

~-~-~-~-~-~

After an Oregon pimp was arrested for repeatedly stomping on the face of a john who wouldn't pay up, the pimp filed suit against Nike for not including a warning label on his shoes. At the hearing, however, a jaded judge threw out the case and instructed the bailiff to staple a warning label to the pimp's forehead.

~-~-~-~-~-~

CNN is reporting that Governor Chris Christie has been spotted in the Express Lane at a Trenton Walmart with eleven items in his cart. This disturbing revelation comes directly on the heels of CNN's two-night documentary, *Chris or Anti-Chris?*, when the American public learned that Jersey's Governor often peeks at the crossword puzzle solution, forgets to turn off his cellphone at the theatre, and occasionally leaves the nearly empty milk carton in the fridge.

~-~-~-~-~-~

Despite all the controversy, the new season of *Duck Dynasty* began this week. Rumor has it that the 2014 season will include network-nudged efforts to cater to America's changing mores. For example:

- Phil will join the local Rotary and fall in love with a gay retailer
- Willie will raise *Duck Commander's* minimum wage to $1.25
- Miss Kay will embrace low-carb, gluten-free recipes, and suddenly die

- During his monthly bath, Uncle Si will snort bath salts, kick a man to death, and then sue Nike

~-~-~-~-~-~

Late yesterday, MSNBC was forced to retract its story alleging that New Jersey's Governor Chris Christie -- for purposes of political revenge -- had personally positioned a bunch of traffic cones to snarl commuter traffic on the George Washington Bridge.

In a mid-day news presser, the Governor blamed the entire mess on miscommunication, claiming he had simply reneged during a game of bridge.

After the press conference, the rarely reverend Al Sharpton, MSNBC's poster boy for unmanaged hypertension, demanded Christie apologize for using the racially insensitive term 'renege.'

~-~-~-~-~-~-~-~-~-~-~

I know. I know. Tough game, huh?

Today's news? Or utter nonsense? It just keeps getting more and more difficult to tell the difference.

But one thing's for sure: we want to keep an eye on this Chris Christie guy. I mean, look at the facts: after being alerted of an abuse of power by his staff, not only did he *not* try to cover it up, but within 24 hours he had fired those responsible, had taken full responsibility as head of his administration, and had held a two-hour, no-holds-barred Q&A press conference.

Clearly, the man is out of control.

Gullible's Travels

Count, chant, and what? Oh, yeah. Breathe.

<>~<>~~~~~~~~~~<>~<>~~~~~~~~~~<>~<>

Okay, gather round, everybody. Here's another tip from our popular series, How Not To Get Slapped By Strangers!

Tip #63: if you ever *do* manage to fully align your seven chakras, don't go to the movies. Remember - once those chakras are synced up, your aura's gonna be radiating like crazy, and it's distracting during the romantic scenes.

(Knock it off with the chanting, too.)

One of the advantages...okay, one of the side-effects of social media is this: all of us are now exposed to every single crazy person in the world. Before the internet, we only ever heard about the tin-foil-hat crowd when they made headlines, usually as part of some messy public disturbance involving too many combustibles and not enough clothes.

But now, every whack biscuit with intermittent internet access and an agenda has her/his own facebook page. Dog lovers, dog haters, dog whisperers, dog therapists, three-headed dog worshipers. Cat aficionados, catfish noodlers, bird watchers, pot-bellied pig personal trainers. Men who like men, short men who like tall women, women who like men who used to be women, people who think Geraldo Rivera should have his own show. (okay, I made that part up)

There are facebook pages for werewolves, blog hops for zombies, and support groups for obese transgendered vampires (Balkan, Aryan, or Cajun). There are groups that argue over the plot holes in *Star Wars*, apparently unaware that *Star Wars* didn't really happen. (Alec Guinness never completed his NASA training.)

And then there are the gurus.

Facebook is positively dripping with dharma merchants, each hawking guaranteed gateways to the next level of consciousness: shamans, psychics, and healers; tarot masters, mind readers, and crystal sellers; Yogi posers and Boo-Boo menders; tellers of fortunes and diviners of futures.

For example, there's Angel, the self-proclaimed Urban Shaman, who hails from that most sacred of cities; that eternal soul-focusing cradle of the spiritual cosmos - Pittsburgh.

Angel, according to Angel, is a scholar, a psychic, a master of the Tarot, and a priest of the Goddess Oya. (Oya, from the Mesoamerican Yiddish 'oy' - roughly translated as "*man*, are these suburban white women gullible or *what*?")

At Angel's facebook page, you can schedule your very own personal Tarot reading - assuming you're so desperate for a reading that you'd go to Pittsburgh to get it. (if you can't work out a visit, Angel offers a Skype-based personal reading, for a personal fee, guaranteed to cleanse your aura *and* your wallet)

On the day I visited Angel's facebook page, he was offering free recorded horoscopes as a marketing teaser. I listened to a little of mine (Libra), and quickly discovered why the advice was free. Witness:

~-~-~-~-~-~

If a new romantic interest enters your life at this time, it may not be for long.
As a single guy in his 50s, I did not need to be told this.

If an interest stays around, that means you have found a soul-mate.
Either that, or I'm keeping her in a cage in the basement.

Relationships that start under Uranus are usually not long-lasting.
Nope. Not a chance I'm touching *that* one. Sometimes you just have to move away from the joke.

~-~-~-~-~-~

As a supplement to his Tarot readings, Angel sells candles (the candles are personally blessed at, you know, his sacred altar, you know, there in downtown Pittsburgh) as well as jewelry that creates a magical aura when worn, as long as you define "magical aura" as your finger turning green.

Angel also sells necklaces that gather strength when he places them on top of his santos.

Yeah, I just bet they do.

But despite Angel's commanding grasp of relationships among middle-aged Librans, he's strangely silent when it comes to the other hot topic among online gurus - how to get one's chakras all lined up. (maybe alignment advice is reserved for Angel's paying customers)

As best as I can tell without writing Angel a check, chakras are points along your spine (you should have seven chakras, unless you've had your spine removed for political reasons). These pesky chakras, when properly aligned, cause your aura to glow. And let's face it, guys - who needs a dull aura?

"Hi, Susie. Wanna go out sometime?"
"Gee, Bobby, I don't know. I can barely visualize your aura."
"I have a trust fund."
"Let's roll, sailor!"

(Let's hope they didn't meet under Uranus.)

So. Here's how you align your chakras, according to one Chakra Alignment facebook page:

- Count up from 1 to 7, pause.
- Count down from 7 to 1, give thanks.

- Soon, your auric emissions will start to radiate pure, bright White Light. (requires 2 AA batteries, sold separately)
- Remember to breathe throughout this exercise.

That's a little spooky. When you have to remind somebody to breathe, maybe their aura's not the only dim thing in their résumé.

Equally frightening - the followers themselves. Here are a few of *their* comments:

~-~-~-~-~-~

Woo hoo! I just received my chakra set!
The chakra set. In case you can't count to seven on your own.

Add real colour therapy to this meditation and you'll receive a profound result.
Just don't forget what number you're on. And remember to breathe.

This next transitional shift is ruled by the Aqurian Age.
Seriously? Aqurian Age? Here's a tip, Aura Boy: before you babble on in your area of expertise, first learn to spell the buzz words.

Cool nice,,,wow pwde ihatang na nimo,,,nko ky red na da,,,
Apparently, this guy's aura mojo started kicking in right around the word 'wow.'

I'll be broadcasting blessings from my home TV studio. So stay tunned.

Be sure your cable company supports fine tunning.

I AM interested in the Sri bite with apophylite.
The God of Moses is a fan of apophylite? Now *that's* an endorsement.

Realgar is used to go into the subconscious and heal past traumas where memories have been suppressed.
Realgar is a very tiny guru with a certificate from the Burbank Online University of Memory Suppression. She is discreet, non-judgmental, and almost never permanently damages a subconscious.

Folks, this crystal is highly poisonous - NEVER handle one of these without gloves.
Why, they're nearly as dangerous as those new light bulbs.

All the candles are blessed by Angel, a santero priest.
So if you're ever in Pittsburgh, and your candles start sneezing, give Angel a call.

And don't forget to breathe.

Rose Bowling for Dollars

Which one's the "gay marriage" float? Oh. Never mind.

<>~<>~~~~~~~~~~<>~<>~~~~~~~~~~<>~<>

Every year's end, it happens. No, not another "Die Hard" sequel. It's the BCS: the college football bowl season -- a heavily-broadcasted intercollegiate tournament that will decide next year's team rankings via the time-tested statistical method of students flying to another State and drinking all the beer that exists in that time zone.

Just before Christmas all across America, colleges, universities, and snack food conglomerates come together for a coordinated barrage of commercials, stadium sponsorships, and hotel discounts, interspersed with the occasional thirty seconds of actual football action.

The commercials never really change all that much - the cars a little newer, the models a little younger, the snack chips now have 17% more flavor. (precise 'flavor' measurements provided by the International Society of Obviously Non-Quantifiable Measurements)

One of this year's car commercials is worth mentioning, though, if for no other reason than its tenacious stamina. This ubiquitous ad kept popping up all season, several times an hour, over and over, game after game after game. Not a particularly *effective* ad: I don't even remember what *kind* of car it was: it was small; it was red; that's all I know. But the "plot" went like this: some collagen-lipped twit is late for a meeting - or maybe a snack chip commercial - so, naturally, she drives up an angled overpass support and lands on top of a commuter train. (see "Die Hard" sequel)

But this is America, land of the guilt-free and home of the depraved. So, in order to shield the car maker from possible legal action by pathologically ignorant stunt driver wannabes (*"Hey, y'all, watch this!"*), their lawyers made the car company superimpose this caption during the ad:

Fantasy. Do not attempt. Cars cannot jump on trains.

Seriously.

Apparently, there are as-yet unincarcerated bipeds out there who might try this stunt.

I live in a constant fear of being seated at a dinner party next to someone that stupid.

The other aspect of bowl season that's changing - or, perhaps better put, intensifying - is corporate sponsorships of the bowl games themselves. It's out of control. Once upon a time, we had the Rose Bowl, the Sugar Bowl, the Cotton Bowl. Nice, simple nouns. But now, every stadium, every bowl game, is as brand-branded as a NASCAR front-runner. The *Allstate* Sugar Bowl. The *Tostitos* Fiesta Bowl. The *TaxSlayer.com* Gator Bowl, played at Wells Fargo Free Checking Field and sponsored by the Federal Reserve's Quantitative Easing.

Imagine where this kind of thing leads...

- The Q-Tip Cotton Swab Bowl
- The Dr. Scholl's Odor-Eater Loafer Insert Bowl
- Johnny Rizzo's Discount Tire & Fan Belt Emporium Bowl
- Mr. Clean's Wipe & Dust Bowl
- The Martha White Enriched Self-Rising Semolina Family Economy Package Bowl
- The Turf-Guard Slug-And-Mildew-Resistant Sod Bowl
- The TaxDragonSlayer Atavism Bowl & Debtors Prison
- Big Tony's Downtown Mixed Gender Gymnasium, Herbal Juice Bar & Drive-Thru STD Clinic Bowl
- The Toyota Fossil Fuel Independence Bowl (*brought to you by the Toyota Priapus - the only car that charges itself!*)

(Whew. What a mouthful...my hands are out of breath.)

And then there's the swag; at least, I *guess* there's swag. I mean, if Martha White Flour is sponsoring a bowl game, some svelte Martha White Flour delegate will be on hand handing out free flour samples, right? (except in Miami, where fans would be trying to snort the samples)

So, for your halftime pleasure, we've stirred together all the sponsors and commercials, the teams and the fans, the announcers and the referees, added a pinch of chilled snarcasm, and half-baked it. Mmm!

And now, let's sample some of the things we heard (or might as well have heard) during the college football bowl season.

~-~-~-~-~-~

"Next up on ESPN, the eagerly anticipated Franklin American Mortgage Music City Bowl. Each lucky member of the winning team will receive a boxed CD set, the well-avoided 'Slim Whitman Rocks the Early Beatles,' and 20% off closing costs."

"North Carolina handily topped Cincinnati in the Belk Bowl. Players and coaches received a lifetime supply of cufflinks; in other words, two."

"Later tonight, the AutoZone Liberty Bowl. Randomly selected fans will each get a set of tire chains, but they have to promise, at some point, to set the tires free."

"Here's an update from our sports desk in the Bronx: it looks like Notre Dame will head home the victor in the New Era Pinstripe Bowl."

(Editor's Note: we're sorry, but we don't have a joke to insert here. There's nothing we could offer that would be funnier than just saying "New Era Pinstripe Bowl.")

"Aw, I do not believe it! *Another* penalty? Where did the Orange Bowl find these referees? Some kind of Moose Club lottery? Man, the *Olympics* didn't have this many flags!"

"Tomorrow night in Arizona, Baylor faces UCF in the Tostitos Fiesta Bowl. We'll be bringing you that game direct from Phoenix, where it's currently 165 degrees...but, as they like to say here in Phoenix, it's a *dry* heat. By the way: we're receiving reports that a few UCF players are 'recovering' from too much Phoenix-style fiesta-ing...but, as they like to say here, it's a *dry* heave."

"Welcome to the 2013 Chick-fil-A Bowl, proudly boycotted by those intolerant tolerance warriors at GLAAD! We're happy to be here; as you probably heard, this year's game was almost cancelled after someone from Chick-fil-A corporate misread a memo and thought Duke was playing some team named Texas S&M."

"For tomorrow's TaxSlayer.com Gator Bowl, analysts are claiming Georgia is 11 points better than Nebraska, on a neutral field. That may explain all these Cornhusker fans who've been tossing partisan liberals into the stadium."

"Sunday, be sure to tune in for the GoDaddy Bowl! We have no idea who's playing, but it doesn't matter. We're just here for the halftime show. If GoDaddy's *off-season* ads are any indication, this should be a wardrobe malfunction that'd cause Cotton Mather to soul-kiss Lady Gaga."

"Well, this is a first. Here in the Orange Bowl, a referee has just penalized one of the other referees."

"Tonight's Alamo Bowl is brought to you by Valero, which is a famous song by Ravel and Bo Derek. As you know, MSNBC had tried to buy the Alamo Bowl sponsorship, but their offer was rejected after MSNBC management kept demanding the field have only a left sideline."

"Sports fans - the long, long wait is over! Today at 3pm, finally...finally!...it's the AdvoCare V100 Bowl. Members of the winning team will each receive a year's supply of Herbal Cleanse, not to mention receiving a very wide berth from passersby on public sidewalks."

"Good evening, folks, and welcome to the Allstate Sugar Bowl, for tonight's battle between Oklahoma and Alabama! We're glad to be here in the New Orleans Superdome, which smells much better than it did back when George Bush caused that hurricane."

"Well, that, um...that was the halftime show from the Orange Bowl. Whew - and we thought the *referees* were bad. We...um...nobody up here in the booth knows who that band was...thankfully...but it was kind of like what you'd hear if U2 got severely-medicated and then married the last-place entry from "Austin's Got Talent," accompanied by several hundred nondescript line dancers."

"This year, the Heart of Dallas Bowl will be played in the Cotton Bowl, but the Cotton Bowl will be played in the AT&T Stadium. In a related story, the Hyundai Sun Bowl was actually played *in the Sun Bowl.* We're guessing somebody in Logistics got fired over *that* one."

~-~-~-~-~-~

Pretty dismal, all in all. But the worst news is yet to come. The bowl season is also a marker: the final games of the college football season. And we know what comes next...

Televised league bowling.

Sticks and Stones Are Words, Too

Boy, you can not say that again!

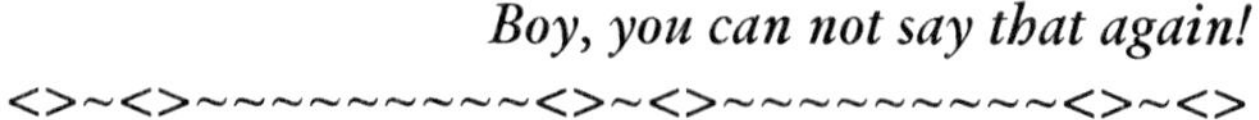

Oh, good. As if us aging single guys didn't have enough social pressure already, now there's an official way to correctly misspell words.

Srsly.

Yes, the vowel-phobic abbreviation *srsly* (short for *seriously*) is now an acceptable word -- along with other Scrabble-challengers, like *derp, twerking,* and *fauxhawk* -- thanks to the definition deans at Oxford Dictionary, the world's only lexicon named after a shoe.

That rush-rush shortcut and others, like 2011's *LOL* and *OMG*, are forever part of the English language, now that Oxford has added them as new coinage. So "srsly" is suddenly kosher in public and private communication (email), social media (#tweets), and most importantly, timeless word games (scrbl).

Editor's Note: we appreciate that there may be a few digital-age holdouts out there ... people who aren't necessarily up to speed on online argot ... people who may be clinging to twisted, regressive hobbies, like reading, or going outdoors, or even (!) communicating face-to-face.

No worries. For the social media acronym-challenged, here's a partial primer:

- SRSLY: seriously
- LOL: laughing out loud
- SRSLYLOL: I'm bipolar
- BFF: best friend forever
- BFD: something Joe Biden blurts, forgetting there's an open mike
- IMHO: in my humble opinion
- IMHFO: Joe Biden saying 'in my humble opinion'
- OMG: omigod
- I: Barack Obama saying 'omigod'
- ROTFL: rolling on the floor laughing
- ROFL: same thing, but I was in a hurry and didn't have time to type 't'
- ROFLMAO: still laughing, but so much so that I've actually begun shedding body parts
- NPIHIDAYCUOTAIMHO: not particularly interesting; however, I did appreciate your clever use of the acronym 'in my humble opinion'
- TLDR: too long - didn't read
- ObamaCare: TLDR

And here are the arcane words also added this year:

- derp: foolishness or stupidity
- fauxhawk: a Mohawk-style haircut, usually found atop the skull of some neck-tattooed kid with nose jewelry and well-founded corporate dreams of starting at the bottom and then working his way down
- twerking: a complex word, loosely defined as "extremely suggestive public dancing performed by a socially-confused, nearly-clothed female singer who apparently got a tongue transplant from a cow." (see *derp*)

As you've probably heard, the Oxford gang's top new word for 2013 is *selfie*. Briefly, a *selfie* is a self-portrait; in practice, however, a selfie is a blurry, badly-composed smartphone self-photo, usually snapped as the subject poses in front of a bathroom mirror while wearing casual, if not downright questionable, fashions.

It can be a private or public bathroom - the selfie addict doesn't care. A person may have a single selfie, or thousands. Generally speaking, the more selfies a person has, the less you want to be near them. (Not that they want to be around you, either -- if a person posts several hundred pictures of themselves, they've reached the point where they see other people and think 'ottoman.') Girls in selfies tend to either smile politely, or threaten to twerk. Guys tend to try to look evil and make stupid little gang signs with their hands. (see *derp*)

Interestingly, while Team Oxford were busily adding new words to our national vocabulary, American educators were just as diligently *removing* words that have fallen out of (their) favor. For example, the NYC Department of Education has come up with some fifty words/phrases that might somehow manage to possibly be offensive -- to anyone, in any place, at any time, ever -- as if the Constitution had enumerated our inalienable rights as life, liberty, and never getting our feelings hurt.

For example, *Halloween* is troubling because it suggests paganism. (I guess *Christmas* is targeted because it doesn't.) You can't say *birthday* because birthdays aren't celebrated by Jehovah's Witnesses (though I haven't heard any ruling on *pamphlet*). The list also includes phrases that might offend Creationists (*dinosaur*) or that might offend evolutionists (*Joe Biden*).

Also included are words or topics that might (gasp!) make students feel discontent: words that suggest wealth are excluded because they might make kids feel jealous; similarly, *poverty* appears on the 'forbidden phrases' list (the Life Nannies recommend the kinder, more abstract *Mercedes-challenged*).

Some particularly gifted morons even want to shield America's brittle kiddies, not only from any potentially painful discussion of things they may already be exposed to (*divorce*, *disease*, *Andrew Weiner*), but from things the kids might never have personally experienced (*oceans*, *volcanoes*, *funny episodes of 'Saturday Night Live'*).

Apparently this neurotic Nanny State thinking goes like this: it's not fair to present test questions about the ocean to a child who's never been to an ocean. What a load of derp. Lots of kids haven't been to France. Should we hide French people, too? Okay, bad example. It would be like saying you can't ask

Andrew Weiner any questions about wearing pants. Okay, bad example.

And besides...look. If a land-bound lad is old enough to figure out how to put on socks, but doesn't know what an *ocean* is, maybe "hurt feelings" isn't really that family's biggest concern. What say we just hold that future Congressman back a grade? I mean, what's the rush? Prisons are already overcrowded.

Other words or phrases that educators say should be banned:

- animal shelters (too traumatic)
- nuclear weapons (too violent)
- running away (unless it's France)
- sports jargon (unless the sport is "running away from nuclear weapons")
- vermin (rats, roaches, the IRS)

Worst of all, while we're all bending over backwards to bubble-wrap America's children, America's *adults* continue to devolve ... as evidenced by this online comment from some facebook philosopher opining on the Second Amendment:

"We got to keep the right to bare arms intack."

Srsly.

Thanks For Being A Sad Pencil So Far

Garbled garbage, de-garbled, is still garbage.

<>~<>~~~~~~~~~~<>~<>~~~~~~~~~~<>~<>

Did you hear about the huge security snafu at Nelson Mandela's memorial? A violent psychotic managed to make his way on stage, stood right next to the US President, and started making wild, incomprehensible hand gestures.

But security quickly escorted Joe Biden off the stage.

That's not true, of course. Joe Biden didn't travel to South Africa with the President. He stayed home to attend political fundraisers and swear.

Besides, you can't have both the President *and* the Vice President in the same potentially dangerous situation at the same time. If something bad should happen, Speaker of the House John Boehner would become President, which would cause people to say something *really* bad just happened, which could potentially spin the universe into an endless "something bad just happened" loop.

Beyond the succession of House Speaker, I forget who the Constitution recommends for President, but after a President Boehner, Americans would probably opt to hold elections by armed combat, or reading bird entrails.

I'm just not sure America is ready for a President who cries every time a woman hands him a mallet.

But it is in fact true that, during the service honoring the South African legend, a crazy man managed to get on stage and stand within inches of several important, competent, decisive world leaders, and also Barack Obama.

Allegedly, the man was an interpreter for the deaf. Absolutely, the man had been *hired* to be an interpreter for the deaf. He'd been brought on board and was paid $85 by some clueless, yawning, civil servant, possibly some local functionary from the South African equivalent of the DMV.

What happened next during the Mandela service was this: various agencies, news sources, and social media began getting shouts from viewers across the planet, all of them confusedly asking, "*What the heck is that guy signing?*"

Idiots like me, of course, had no idea that the signer was "speaking" complete gibberish. Sure, I did notice that he seemed to point to his head a lot, but so does that bearded guy who hangs around outside my grocery wearing earflaps, a stained parka, and unmatched tennis shoes.

But experts started noticing it, too. The signer was not signing in any known sign language, including ASL, any of the eleven recognized languages of South Africa, or any of the "finger salutes" used by Americans stuck in freeway traffic or the line at the DMV.

How such a charlatan could ever manage to sneak one past the goalie like that is still a mystery, at least to us on this side of the pond. But let's not pretend that America hasn't been guilty of equally bad judgments. Remember - Americans parents will go their kids' baseball games wearing camo Snuggies. The Terminator was a Governor, Al Franken is a Congressman, and Al Sharpton got his own TV show. With hair like that.

Afterwards, revelations about the bogus signer flew fast and furious. It turns out he'd actually been hired as a sign language interpreter before, about a year earlier, but skated through that gig unchallenged. (I'm guessing it was a convention of caffeine addicts with Attention Deficit Disorder, or some event involving lots of nearly-clothed runway models)

Once the guy had been hauled in, he quickly mounted a unique defense: he claimed that, while interpreting, he'd had a schizophrenic attack.

(As a schizo-burger side-order, he mentioned being further distracted by all the angels he saw descending into the stadium.)

According to a *real* interpreter, one who as a rule doesn't have psychotic hallucinations before lunch and rarely sees angels wafting around the rafters, here's a sample of what the now-famous fake seemed, at one point in Obama's remarks, to have been signing:

"Thanks for being a sad pencil so far."

As reporters begin to munch on this delicious story, more and more of the guy's shifty history began to surface. According to one source, he'd been charged with murder some ten years ago. It's not clear, though, if he ever did any time for that rap, because when asked about the incident, the guy signed:

"Four or three balls of hard color, this is my right temple."

And now, we learn that the bogus interpreter at the Mandela funeral has faced several charges, including rape, murder, and signing a split infinitive. However, when confronted with the allegations, the interpreter haughtily signed:

"Several tall orange is more to a gerbil's omelet leverage."

Of course, at the end of the day, the sad result was that the remarks and tributes made at Mandela's memorial were denied to people with hearing problems, as well as people who are apparently deaf, like Congress, and a woman I used to date.

But the most damning proof that the interpreter ... well, *can't* ... came when he took a stab at signing his way through one of President Tee Time's rah-rah speeches about that fabulously popular involuntary mandate, Obamacare.

This is gonna be hard to believe, but here's what the signer signed:

"If you like your doctor, you can keep your doctor. Period."

Unbelievable. No way. That *can't* be what our President actually said.

Maybe Obama should hire this former/future felon as Press Secretary. Imagine what you could accomplish with a guy whose hands have a mouth like that...

I'm Dreaming of a White Santa

A duck. A fox. A donkey. It must be Christmas!

<>~<>~~~~~~~~~~<>~<>~~~~~~~~~~<>~<>

Earth. Christmas 2013. A full year has now passed since the Mayan Apocalypse didn't happen, possibly due to the fact that their calendar was a rock. Or maybe the Mayans got a last-minute health care exemption.

So we're still here. But, from the Milky Way's perspective, was it worth it? Let's review.

In America, shoppers are stabbing each other over who gets the Dollar Store's only remaining Peace Sign necklace. In China, acres of acne-aged Asians are hacking the Pentagon and hocking iPhone knockoffs. In Iran, government-backed fanatics are spinning up nuclear weapons like under-quota used car salesmen at month's end. And North Korea's Kim du jour just had his adored Dennis Rodman declared an official People's Short Person.

Madness. And what's headlining in the US news media?

- A ditzy news-show talking head who joked that Jesus and Santa are white people
- A self-described "redneck" duck hunter from the Louisiana backwoods who ... now hang on to something ... doesn't condone homosexuality

Good grief. How low can we go? Next thing you know, we'll be fixating on the First Lady's bangs or something. So let's move to a more edifying topic, one that can actually be of some benefit to you and your family:

Bad Christmas Songs!

Following is a list of some real corkers. I lined them up in no particular order, and I won't deign to judge which is the worst, or the least worst. However, in the interest of good, clean research, it's worth noting that one song is *not* included - "The Christmas Shoes" - a "*Please Make It Stop!*" ditty so overwhelmingly merciless that I wrote an entire column just about it.

Some of these songs I've known all my life, some I'd never heard of before doing some internet research on "stupid Christmas songs," thanks to Al Gore's wonderful invention (hair gel).

Let's begin.

Please, Daddy, Don't Get Drunk This Christmas

Last year I was seven. Now I'm nearly eight, as you can see.

You came home, half past eleven, and fell down underneath the Christmas tree.

We don't know what was going on in John Denver's life when he unleashed this merry little number in 1973, but we can't help but notice the 1974 release of "I Saw Mommy Suing Santa Claus For Irreconcilable Differences."

It's Christmas Every Day

As far as we can tell, this holiday video from England is about a wannabe musician trying to get a producer to listen to his demo tape. Along the way, there's an exploding turkey. There are twins wearing tinsel boas. And the wannabe gets electrocuted by his guitar. So it ends well.

I Want a Hippopotamus for Christmas

This was frightening. It was JonBenet Ramsey in black & white, but with some weird zoo animal fetish.

1953. The Ed Sullivan Show. A rabidly-coached ten-year-old named Gayla Peevey performed this tightly-staged number about a young girl who would be satisfied with nothing but an aggressive, two-ton African water horse.

The Sullivan show's set was a front porch; the skit's extras were two pre-puberty Stepford Wives who never said a word during the entire song - they just sat on the steps and jacked their heads back and forth, keeping time during disturbing lyrics like this:

There's lots of room for him in our two-car garage
I'll feed him there and wash his hair and give him a massage

Of course, in the 50s, child protection services were a bit more lenient about little girls who wanted to rub down vicious aquatic mammals.

Walking In A Winter Wonderland

This well-known favorite is mostly harmless. But responsible clergy can't ignore this lyric:

In the meadow we can build a snowman and pretend that he is Parson Brown.

I don't know this for a fact, but I'm guessing your wedding may not be legally binding if the vows were exchanged in front of a guy who's melting. Either way, it can't be good luck if the ceremony's pastor is related to the reception's ice sculpture.

Minnie and Santa

From her feral, fetchingly-titled holiday album "Merry Christmas...Have a Nice Life" Cyndi Lauper gifts us a bawdy melody about a wiggly tramp who has the hots for Santa. I'll spare you the details, but Minnie even manages to make milk and cookies filthy.

Christmas Is Coming

Christmas is coming, the goose is getting fat
Please put a penny in the old man's hat

We're not sure where this song came from...even Wikipedia is too embarrassed to discuss this one. But it obviously originated during a particularly low point in England's history, a time when men's fashion was directly impacted by obese geese.

It gets worse.

Christmas is coming, the egg is in the nog
Please give a friendly man a friendly dog

"*The egg is in the nog.*" Please. Man, the things those Anglo-Saxons wouldn't do to rhyme a couplet.

Misty

Eclectic British singer Kate Bush wakes up on a winter night to find a snowman in her bed.

As one might.

She asks him to leave.

Eventually.

Frosty the Snowman

And speaking of smiling snowmen, there's this perennial about a snowman who becomes animated, though not in a way that would make Kate Bush dust and vacuum.

To be honest, it's an okay tune. There's nothing fundamentally wrong with the *song*...it's the song's *delivery system* that's potentially a problem. When Frosty gets lobbed at us by Burl Ives, what's wanted next is an intervention. Burl Ives at Christmas is an unusually cruel thing to do to a person. It should be banned outright, by international treaty if necessary, and I think all reasonable governments would agree.

Grandma Got Run Over by a Reindeer

This allegorical argument for mandatory family planning was originally performed by a couple called Elmo & Patsy.

We should've known to run when we saw "Elmo & Patsy."

Santa Claus Goes Straight to the Ghetto

A collaboration by Snoop Doggy Dogg, Nate Dogg, Diz Dillinger, Bad Azz, Tray Dee, and Bing Crosby.

I'm joking, of course. Bing thinks Bad Azz is chanky.

On the first day of Christmas, my homeboy gave to me
A sack of the crazy glue and told me to smoke it up slowly

Yeah, I know. That lyric required a *collaboration.*

We probably don't want to be in the room when the nine ladies dancing arrive.

Christmas at K-Mart

The mood ring counter is all aglow.

Here's what you need to know: that's the song's *best* line.

Dominick the Christmas Donkey

Okay, I lied. I *did* save the worst for last.

Dominic the Christmas Donkey is an audio aberration first thrust upon our species in 1960 by a guy named Lou Monte.

I don't really trust myself to discuss this song. Whenever it ambushes me on the radio, I have a reaction very similar to Hannibal Lector with low blood sugar.

But after doing some more research in Al Gore's hair gel, I began to see a pattern. Maybe Mr. Monte couldn't help himself. I mean, it didn't stop with Dominic. Look at what *else* the guy wrote:

Pepino the Italian Mouse
Pasqual the Italian Pussy-Cat
Paulucci the Italian Parrot
Paul Revere's Horse (Ba-Cha-Ca-Loop)

So, in the spirit of the season, let's all just settle down. Let's not worry about whether Santa is white, particularly in light of the fact that *Santa doesn't exist.* And let's not worry about whether a camo-clad bearded guy in a duck blind owns a copy of *Brokeback Mountain.* We're all part of one big humanity stew. We've more in common with each other than we sometimes see.

After all...who knew Paul Revere was a Sicilian!

Stark Raving Naked

Can cold weather fight crime?

<>~<>~~~~~~~~~~<>~<>~~~~~~~~~~<>~<>

Here's a free fashion tip, Single Guys: when going for that unique, just-right international look, don't stop with just the turban and heels -- round out your stunning ensemble with some actual *clothes*.

Especially if you're trying to be stunning in South Georgia.

Recently, someone sent me an article about a guy who'd been arrested, in Georgia, for indecent exposure. At least, that was the *initial* charge. Let's review the particulars:

- Neighbors reported a suspicious-looking guy.
- Exhibit A: the guy was wearing a turban
- True, that's not illegal. Even in South Georgia.
- Exhibit B: he was also wearing high heels
- Okay, now we may need to get a ruling from the booth.

- Turban, heels, and ... nothing else.
- Hard to argue with that one. In fact, if I was raking the yard and some unelected whack dashed by wearing nothing but heels and a turban, I'd go with "suspicious-looking" too. And then I'd sell the house.
- It was at this point that "the law" got involved. As you might have guessed, there are all manner of ordinances that frown upon turbaned men of the male persuasion sprinting in the altogether.
- When first observed by local deputies, the peeled perp was trying to pull on a pair of pink panties.
- To tastefully accomplish that feat, he was hiding behind an allegedly suspicious-looking tree.
- As one might.
- When the police approached this leafless Adam, the Sikh-like sicko ran away.
- As one might.

Okay, let's review. You've got a naked man in a turban, almost wearing women's undergarments, running from rural police in South Georgia.

In heels.

I'd have paid ten dollars to see that.

Here's some more from the article:

- According to the final police report, Captain Stark was inexplicably carrying a pair of sweatpants. Probably didn't go with the heels.

- You know, for a naked person, this guy sure had lots of clothes.
- During his assuredly chilly flight, the alleged man allegedly dropped an alleged Crown Royal bag.
- The Crown Royal bag contained ... wait for it ... drugs.
- According to the locals, this was not the first time Bare-skinned Boy had been arrested. In fact, this wasn't even the first time he'd been arrested *this week*.
- But it *was* the first time he'd been arrested without any pockets.
- Earlier in the week, the guy had been arrested at a local shopping center, after jumping a curb in his car. The police charged him with ... wait for it ... DUI.
- But that day the man ran away and escaped, possibly because during *that* incident he was wearing sensible shoes.
- This time, however, the police caught him. There was a brief struggle, and that horrible 'brief' pun was not my fault. I'm just reporting the news.
- Among other things, the allegedly shivering man was charged with public indecency, drug possession with intent to distribute, obstructing an officer, and transporting underage sweatpants across state lines.
- (The Baron of Barren was also charged with something called "failure to maintain lane," but personally, we think that's just cold. That's just piling on. This guy's got enough misery without dragging the DMV into it.)
- Worst of all, the entire unattired crime spree took place on a Sunday. (remember, we're in South Georgia)

On one level, you gotta admire a guy who can fit that much crime into a single Sunday's morning jog, and handle the chill. On the other hand, it's hard to have much respect for a man with such shallow fashion sense; even the most inexperienced nearly nude cross-dressing Southern streaker knows that sweatpants and turban is *not* a good look.

Fashion faux pas aside, however, the Perambulating Naked Man might have gotten away with just a warning if it weren't for that Crown Royal bag.

I'm sure you've seen a Crown Royal bag, even if you didn't *realize* it was a Crown Royal bag. You know the trademark purple felt, the yellow drawstring, the faint and faintly-familiar singed aroma of an Allman Brothers concert.

This is where our unclothed cross-country rookie slipped up. I mean, let's face it: anybody over the age of eleven knows that there are only three things people ever, ever keep and carry in Crown Royal bags:

- drugs
- their multi-decade penny collection
- drugs

Small-town cops are busy, too. They don't have time to just screech around town, arresting every turban-topped trouser-free man they see hanging out on the streets near schoolyards, retirement homes, and nuclear facilities.

"Bill, check out *that* guy, behind the tree."
"And?"

"Seems to be a little wardrobe-challenged. Just sayin'."
"Well, he *is* naked, but I don't see any Crown Royal bags."
"Yeah, it's probably nothin'. Wonder what's up with the sweatpants."
"Please. With those heels?"
"Point taken."
"Nice turban."

Of course, the bare jogger report ended the way these small-town breaking crime reports always end - with this sentence:

It's unclear if [insert arrested person's name] has an attorney.

I don't know why the papers always add that tag. Maybe it's just insider tchotchke; some nearly-subtle suckle from the family that owns the newspaper, tossed to the local ambulance chasers.

I'd imagine that your average lawn-dashing clothing minimalist doesn't think to line up legal counsel in advance. Besides, no in dishabille Dillinger needs an allegation of premeditation.

You know how it is: it's early morning, you've only yet had the one coffee, you're planning the morning's nearly nekkid sexual deviance - it's easy to get caught up selecting stilettos, auxiliary sweatpants, and escape routes. Some details are bound to slip your mind.

It's unclear if the sweatpants have an attorney.

Of House Mice and Cave Men

Yes, we're all related. No, you can't come for Christmas.

<>~<>~~~~~~~~~~<>~<>~~~~~~~~~~<>~<>

I was on facebook the other day, checking to see what the head of the NSA was planning to cook for dinner, when somebody posted a picture of Rae Dawn Chong from the movie *Quest for Fire*. In the shot, she was hunkered down by a normal Cro Magnon fire, wearing your standard-issue Cro Magnon body paint and naked as Nancy Pelosi's agenda. Naturally, I averted my gaze, mostly so I could click the "more" link.

The link led to a webpage promising eight incredible facts I might not know about human evolution, though I'm guessing that most people who clicked "more" were more likely hoping for incredible facts about Rae Dawn Chong.

But I kept reading. I was in no rush to get back to facebook; after all, the NSA guy was having soup...again.

I knew immediately that I was in good hands, surrounded by solid, stable science - in a sidebar on the webpage, the author also recommended such other "Don't miss!" articles as these:

- A plane crash in Argentina that's being blamed on a UFO
- A challenge to Americans to stop keeping eggs in the fridge
- A library that claims its copy of *Fifty Shades of Grey* has herpes
- China's pending baby boom (I blame Argentinian UFOs for carpet-bombing Beijing with copies of Fifty Shades of Grey.)

However, I *will* give the website five bonus points for not mentioning Sasquatch.

And then there's this little résumé bullet point about the article's author: she's written a book on how humans will survive a mass extinction.

Hmm. After a mass extinction, I'd always assumed there wouldn't *be* any survivors. I thought 'no survivors' was what mass extinction *meant.*

So hop aboard and let's look at some of these incredible facts about you and me. (well, *you*, anyway ... I'm still not sure I belong in this research)

WARNING: While the article is moving, please keep your suspension of disbelief firmly fastened at all times. And please keep your hands inside the article until the research comes to a complete stop.

Humans navigated the Indian Ocean in boats 50,000 years ago

The author bases this "fact" on timing: the alleged appearance of humanoids in Australia (if I have my math right, this would've been 49,999 years ago, late on a Wednesday). I mean, people had to get there *somehow* - it's not like Australia was populated by South American UFOs. Probably.

But even the *author* admits that such a feat shouldn't have worked. Then she quipped that the boat journey would've been the Paleolithic equivalent of humans flying to the moon in a tin can. This is an example of what evolutionary scientists would call 'bar humor,' or, to use the layman's term for it, 'lonely.'

Humans have incredibly low genetic diversity

In case you didn't already know ... or, much less likely, care ... low genetic diversity is an evolutionary scientist-type measurement, based on another measurement called the "effective population size." At this point the article began to get a little technical, but I think the measurements are calculated by computing the total body mass index of either

4) Polynesia, or
5) Toronto Mayor Rob Ford

The major research cited on this topic was done using wild house mice; you know, since we're dealing with humans and everything. Or maybe Mayor Ford just barked a bit when the lab brought up that "dissection" business.

Ultimately, the point here seems to be this: humans are a lot like other humans.

Ooh. I smell Nobel Prize.

You may be part Neanderthal

In other words, science can now prove that our cavemen ancestors already had monster trucks and cage wrestling.

Additionally, there is some anecdotal evidence of European cross-breeding between French Cro Magnons and post-African Neanderthals, but that's to be expected in a culture dominated by knuckle-walking guys with monster trucks and Rae Dawn Chong running around flicking Zippo lighters all over the place. Plus, they're French.

Homo sapiens has had a culture for less than 50,000 years

Apparently, scientists can now carbon-date the monster trucks. Meanwhile, French Cro Magnon neo-Neanderthals are double-dating the carbon-dating.

The human population crashed about 80,000 years ago

I'm not sure what the scientists meant by 'crash,' but I'm pretty sure they weren't talking about the trucks. Maybe mankind ran out of South American coffee.

And, lastly, we learn that...

Early human beings left Africa over one million years ago

We know this to be an indisputable fact, because the author has a chart. (Only two types of people use charts: research scientists and politicians. Everybody else is busy actually working.)

The chart's title was "The Human Diaspora" (literal translation: *everybody's Jewish*). It was a flat projection of Earth - yeah, I thought that was funny, too - overlaid with what was either proto-human migratory routes, or the circulatory system of a mollusk. The various veins/routes were color-coded: you know, blue = millions of years ago; red = thousands of years ago; green = sometime late Wednesday.

The chart indicated which out-of-Africa groups went where, and when. All your major migratory players were represented: homo sapiens, homo erectus, homo neanderthalensis, homo depot, Jed Clampett.

An attendant image depicted a collection of humanoid skulls, lined up left to right, oldest to newest; well, smallest to largest, anyway. For all I know, the one on the right was a normal human, and the left-most was an MSNBC anchor.

Actually, the skull on the far left had huge eyes and no bottom jaw. I think I dated her.

In fact, based on the skulls in the photo, if you go back far enough in the fossil record, *nobody* had a bottom jaw. Either that, or they were awfully careless, mandible-wise.

"Honey, be a dear and chew this for me."

"Forgot your jaw at home again, didn't you, Og."
"Oh, give it a rest!"
"Mother warned me not to get involved with a homo ergaster."
"We didn't *have* mothers."
"Oh, yeah."

But here's the author's core "fact" - two million years ago last Wednesday, a band of "brave explorers," who lived in a warm, tropical paradise with wives who looked like Rae Dawn Chong, decided to head north to "seek refuge."

Before, I always thought: Refuge from *what?* National Geographic photojournalists? Homo Pharaoh?

And now, we know who left, and why.

It was Og.

More Things I've Learned from TV

Why SETI started searching elsewhere

<>~<>~~~~~~~~~~<>~<>~~~~~~~~~~<>~<>

Remember the movie *Contact*?

Basically, the story line was this: while searching for intelligent life, a young woman had sex with one of those rare non-celibate televangelists, and then he never returned her calls, so naturally she decided to launch herself into outer space. Then, as often happens, she met a psychotic trillionaire who agreed to pay for the whole project.

Later, after not being assassinated by Gary Busey's brother, she strapped herself into the madman's secret rocket ship, which was allegedly powered by some kind of giant gyroscope (remember - the trillionaire *was* psychotic) and was inexplicably transported to Pensacola, where she chatted with her dead father about various galactic ambiguities, like time-space wormholes, shepherding aliens, and the oddly enduring attraction of potted meat.

Even more inexplicable: although the young woman was in Pensacola for almost ten minutes, not a single mentally unbalanced panhandler hit her up for wine money.

But nestled in amongst all those realistic bits was an interesting subplot: the "listeners" at SETI were all gaga because they had finally received a non-random pattern from something or someone, somewhere in the universe.

And that's when things got weird: the pattern was a bounced-back TV signal that had originated *from Earth* -- Adolph Hitler, broadcasting from the 1936 Olympic Games in Berlin. (spry little Adolph was the hands-on favorite to pick up the gold in the 400-Meter Fascist Dash)

See, according to Carl Sagan, the author of *Contact*, television coverage of the '36 Olympics was the first transmission from Earth powerful enough to make it into outer space (not counting Ethel Merman), so it was the first transmission ever picked up by an extraterrestrial culture. And the way the ETs let us know they were listening was by sending the transmission back to us, because they didn't know how to spell LOL.

Obviously, Earth's leaders were unpleasantly surprised to learn that our intergalactic first impression had been Adolph Hitler. And the news really upset Geraldo Rivera, who wasn't even *born* in 1936 and therefore couldn't inject himself into the story.

Fast-forward to April 2009, and the very first humor column I ever published. And what, you may be asking, but probably not, does my first humor column have to do with a broadcast of the 1936 Olympics? Well, I'll tell you:

- My column was also produced entirely in black and white
- Shortly after writing the column, I conquered Europe
- Like the '36 TV transmission, decades passed by before anybody read the column
- And, like the alien Vegans, even *after* people read it, they didn't get it

No, here's the connection: the first humor column I ever wrote was a simple list, based on a simple idea -- if the only info aliens had about Earth was what they'd seen on television ... especially television commercials ... what assumptions would they make about us?

First of all, I'm guessing the spaceshippers would take one quick, nervous glance at us, drop a couple of bucks on the table, and warp-speed the heck out of here.

But in case there are any newly-arrived aliens, here's an updated list:

- If you buy the wrong car insurance, your girlfriend could end up spending the next Saturday jet-skiing with a small pig.
- Somewhere in America, a house is broken into every fourteen seconds. You'd think that guy would move.
- During college football games, there's a law that requires every sports network to run ads for Doritos, roll-on underarm testosterone, and torque-rich trucks that have a hemi, whatever the heck *that* is.

- Booking a room on a cruise ship can introduce you to all kinds of exciting adventures, including shuffleboard, violent gastrointestinal illness, and running into small islands.
- If America is not careful, a roomful of Chinese students will sit in a dim room, watch a short film, and then collapse the US economy.
- Without trains to deliver things, people wouldn't have nearly as many things. We're not sure who delivered thc trains.
- Korean Air may have the most fantastic in-flight service imaginable, but that's not really gonna matter if you get stuck sitting between ad hoc Ambassador Dennis Rodman and his tattoos.
- Canadian mayors have way more fun than their American counterparts.
- If you buy a particular miracle spray product, you can cut the bottom out of a boat, replace the boat's bottom with a screen door, coat the door with the miracle spray product, and then launch the boat and sit in it without dying. On the down side, the miracle product has the unfortunate side-effect of making you grin like a jackal that's had its nervous system removed.
- America has fifty-seven States, and America's President has visited all of them.
- Joseph A. Bank, the "Buy One, Get Eighteen Free!" men's clothing store, sells stolen merchandise. That's the only possible answer.

- A wildly popular female singer is allowed wear a dress made out of meat, but saying a prayer at a high school football game is too offensive to tolerate.
- At least, I *think* it's a female.

Hopefully, this discussion helped prepare you to be a helpful interstellar ambassador, so you'll be ready to respond on the inevitable day when slimy, eight-armed, two-headed visitors point a death ray at you and demand you take them to our leaders.

If you can find any leaders.

Thank God It's ... Thursday?

How hope & change brought pole dancing to Guam

<>~<>~~~~~~~~~~<>~<>~~~~~~~~~~<>~<>

Well, here we are. It's the first of November, and HealthScare.gov, the world's loneliest website, is now one month old. And during its inaugural thirty days, the website actually worked for nearly eleven whole minutes.

But not in a row.

This may very well be the worst website you ever heard of -- mostly because, in real life, you'd have never heard of it. Nobody but the government would debut a website that sucked this much.

Even by the kindest possible measurement, this thing is a real smeller. It's what a website would look like if a website was starring in a movie directed by Roland Emmerich *and* Cecil B. DeMille.

Let's face it: in some ancient cultures, it wouldn't have been allowed to survive that first month. A mutant this disastrously malformed would've already been plopped down on an ice floe and given a little windward push out to sea, where it would drift into oblivion to join other colossal failures, like the Edsel, and new Coke, and Andrew Dice Clay doing Shakespeare.

Six hundred million taxpayer dollars to build a website that has a dropdown list of available States, and the dropdown list includes the Northern Mariana Islands, the Virgin Islands, and Guam. And then, if you select Guam, you have to throw your computer through a window because the website tells you you're not eligible to use the website. (Let's hope high blood pressure medication is covered in Guam.)

It's the only website in history with a home page that offers four ways to sign up...***and using the website is the second choice.***

Six hundred million taxpayer dollars to build a website, and it doesn't even have a web counter. We think. Because, for the first month, nobody in the government could tell us how many people had been to the website.

You know how to get a web counter, don't you? Of course you do. You get an eight-year-old to Google "free web counter," go to free-web-counter.com, and paste the code. Done.

And the eight-year-old would do it for, oh, four-five hundred million, tops.

But the White House says they have no clue how many visitors. (They say this, of course, while blaming the website's insurmountable crashes on "high volume." Yes, they *do* think we're that stupid. Yes, they do.)

Nor can Obama's crackerjack staff tell us how many people created a HealthScare.gov account, or how many of those people actually signed up, or how many people in Ohio voted after being pronounced legally dead. In fact, the President swears he didn't even know we had a health care website until he read about it on Twitter.

When pressed by the press to give up some hard numbers about HealthScare.gov, the best the government could come up with is this: to their knowledge, nobody attempting to use the website has ever been physically maimed.

But at the core of this hilariously flubbed wealth redistribution scheme, there's one number the White House *has* to admit: in order to generate enough "buyers" so they'll have some wealth to redistribute, HealthScare.gov has to somehow cajole 39,000 people to sign up every day, day in and day out, seven days a week, from now until March 2014.

On day one, they got six.

Not six *thousand*, mind you. Not six *hundred*.

Six. As in all the dwarves except Dopey.

But that's enough *good* news. Let's review some actual anecdotes from HealthScare.gov visitors, shall we?

- Somewhere in Missouri, a forty-seven-year-old single guy was actually able to create a HealthScare.gov account. (Apparently, he mistakenly hit some arcane multi-key combination, triggering a hidden "work" code module.) He entered all the required information, hit 'Submit' and was immediately arrested by Child Protective Services.
- One analysis claims that the HealthScare.gov website has over 500 million lines of code, and that to address all the website's issues, somebody's gonna have to rewrite over 5 million lines of that code. To put things into perspective, the entire Microsoft Windows operating system is only 2 million lines of code, although most of that is "please reboot" messages.
- In fact, the site is so lame that it apparently killed the young female model featured on the original home page. About a week after launch, she suddenly vanished and cannot be located by the combined forces of the international media. It's like she was Osama bin Laden, but with bangs.
- Someone in Long Island who was trying not to bleed to death punched the "Ask a Navigator for help!" button, and was immediately transferred...to a cupcake store. And these are the professionals who are gonna decide if your Aunt Maureen can get a new liver.
- In Guam, officials reported a huge spike in citizens inexplicably shrieking "Whaddaya mean, not eligible?" just before hurling laptops out of windows and onto the streets.
- Somewhere in Delaware, a woman named Judith allegedly saw some actual numbers somewhere on the

website and claims she will, in fact, save money on her health insurance, as long as she stands stock still in her carpeted hallway until she dies or attends a "Shakespeare in the Park" festival featuring Andrew Dice Clay. The White House immediately flew Judith to the Rose Garden for a "HealthScare.gov Victory!" press conference and then appointed her Ambassador to the Northern Mariana Islands.

- Alleged prostitutes are allegedly *thrilled* about HealthScare.gov. According to the internet, it can difficult for, um, independently-employed sex trade entrepreneurs to get health care coverage. Just ask Siouxsie Q, a Bay Area activist who manages a weekly podcast called - and I am not good enough to make this stuff up - The WhoreCast. Siouxsie Q was interviewed while prepping for an ObamaCare registration drive dubbed - again, I am not good enough - dubbed the Healthy Ho's Party.
- (And if you have a pre-existing condition that lasts for more than six hours, please consult your physician immediately.)
- In one poll, 2% of people polled think the implementation of ObamaScare has been "excellent." Yes, that's right: Excellent. I'm guessing these are the people you see walking down the street, wearing several jackets and a fur-lined ear-flap hat in August, gesturing wildly and arguing with a half-empty jar of pickles.
- And finally, as part of a poll in New York, only 22% of doctors say they plan to accept ObamaCare patients. 76% say they plan on moving to Guam, and the remaining 2% are in prison.

Of course, one of the coolest (and under-discussed) things about government-controlled health care is that everybody's gonna get Friday off! Forever! When the Affordable Care Act (that's it's *own* joke) starts punishing employers for hiring 50 full-time employees, even Joe Biden could figure out what happens next:

- nobody will hire more than 49 people
- everybody will be part-time
- nobody will have any discretionary income
- prostitutes will migrate to Guam by the boatload

And if you end up broke? No worries! The Obama will usher you into your new life as a numb, dumb, government-managed ward of The State. You...and the entire American work force.

How can he afford to pay everybody for everything for their whole life?

To quote one of his supporters: "I 'on know. Maybe he got a stash."

At least we *think* it was a supporter. With that kind of résumé-packing intellect, she might be the HealthScare.gov web developer.

Or Siouxsie Q's realtor in Guam.

Voodoo and the Sacrifice Bunt

What is an Arby Eye, anyway?

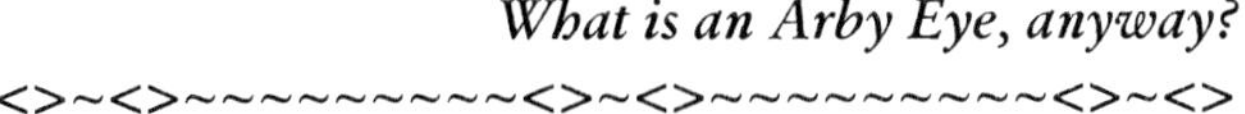

I'm not a big baseball fan. Never was. As a kid I was never any good at the game, I don't own any knickers or knee-high socks, and I don't spit much. Besides, it's hard to get all worked up over a game invented by a guy named Abner.

But now it's October, so I *have* been watching the playoffs and the World Series, because I was born in the 1950s, and so I understand it's my patriotic duty as an American to watch the World Series. In fact, I think it's the law.

Any child of the '50s knows three things:

1) Nobody skips the World Series except godless card-carrying Communists, and college professors.
2) The versatile noun *cheese* can also be a verb, as in "Cheese it, guys! The cops!"
3) You might get the urge to kiss girls. Or you might decide to commit mass murder in a crowded geriatric ward while

drop-kicking blind orphaned kittens. Either way - straight to hell.

So watching the World Series has become an integral part of the American psyche, like getting groped by obese Federal agents at the airport, or paying kidnapper-ransom prices for movie popcorn.

But every year, when I tune in to those end-of-season baseball games, I'm consistently fascinated by Baseball's fascination with statistics. I mean, these people monitor and measure *everything.* They're like the NSA, except they use their own money.

It goes way, way beyond just keeping count of hits, strikes, fouls, errors, steroid indictments, straightforward stuff like that. The baseball world's obsession with statistics is a deeply-seated fixation, blending equal elements of alchemy, voodoo, and superstition. In any particular game, any particular team manager might make tactical decisions because batter X, when facing pitcher Y, gets base hits 20% more times than when facing pitcher Z during night games on alternate Wednesdays or Fridays except when two or more switch-hitting second-basemen have been left on base during a partial lunar eclipse within eight statute miles of a fish taco buffet.

Okay, I exaggerated a little in that example. Nobody has a fish taco buffet.

If you've watched any baseball at all, you're familiar with the dugouts, right? The dugouts are those cheerless-looking sunken shelters where the teams sit on a modified Spanish

Inquisition bench and await their turn to play ball. Inside the dugout, international law mandates that managers and players:

- endlessly gnaw on great huge slugs of chewing gum
- make phone calls to the "bullpen" on circa-1970 wall-phones
- practice spitting

But somewhere below the dugouts, baseball franchises apparently keep cavernous rooms filled with pale, pencil-packing number crunchers, and those milky-eyed scribes track a *staggering* array of ratios, facts, and averages, analyzing each player, scrutinizing every play, and dissecting every game.

They even have a name, these CPA-morphs, these scuttering cave bats: sabermetricians. (an ancient Nordic term, roughly translated as "yet another Brad Pitt vehicle")

And these cave trolls provide the team managers with histories and probabilities for every on-field situation imaginable. What's this pitcher's record against right-handed designated hitters in late innings on artificial turf when there's been a slow hurricane season? How does this batter like fast balls when it's a full count and runners are on second during weekday rush hour? Who's the best second basemen to call on when facing a left-handed starter who has a brutal slider, prefers New York-style pizza, and sucks his teeth in public?

But it's not enough that the managers pore over these numbers. Oh, no. The teams feel the need to share all those suffocating stats with the ball game announcers; you know, those network TV guys with the injection-molded hair, the horrid plaid sport coats, and the Chiclet-sized teeth. These guys are experts at sitting in front of a microphone for 3 to 6 hours and never once shutting up. The networks call this barrage "color commentary." That explains the plaid coats.

So be warned. At any moment during a baseball game, you're in imminent danger of hearing arcane, ear-jarring patois like this:

- It's rare to pitch around a hitter with a two-run lead in a middle inning.
- He's not that good, but Cleveland is seven and one when he's gotten past the first bag.
- Since 1944, 85% of pennants have been clutched by the club that won Game Three.
- In the post season, Saltisambucco has an ERA of 3.2, a 115 OPS in 21 PAs, an IOU that's at least twice that, and eight Arby Eyes.
- Corolla is batting .335 in temperate climates against left-handed Protestant pitchers who've had three or more moles removed by Eastern European dermatologists and who were breast-fed past their bar mitzvah birthday.

And while we're at it, it's worth a quick look at the difference between baseball announcers and their cousins, football announcers. Here's one example:

Baseball

Lost in the weeds, Javiera, a former Aruban coconut weigher, faces the top of the order in the bottom of the sixth, and he can count on some first-hand second-guessing from first and third during the fifth on the Fourth. The kid, who's barely twenty-one years old, needs to buckle down and hurl a down-and-in splitter at Veelander, who is one for five despite having gone .288 in the post-season after rifling a two-run Arby Eye double and then stranding a damage-stemming insurance run from a rally-sparking relief pitcher with an ERA of two-point-double-naught and an IQ of, like, twelve.

Football

It's third and ten. Back to you, Biff.

Mind you: I'm not digging at baseball, just *media coverage* of baseball. I'm only commenting on baseball's jargon - the slang, the argot - and I'm speaking as someone who admittedly doesn't speak baseball. After all, they don't call complicated dialogue "inside baseball" for nothing.

Nor did I come to mock baseball players. Sure, they're all-growed-up men who get paid huge sacks of money for playing games. But there's another group of American adults who do the exact same thing.

We call them the United States Congress. And they can't even *bunt*.

But boy, can they steal.

Postjacking

facebook, revisited

<>~<>~~~~~~~~~~<>~<>~~~~~~~~~~<>~<>

Here's a number to ponder: 1.1 billion. That's one billion, one hundred million. What do you think that Marlon Brando-dwarfing number represents?

a) the running count of Fleetwood Mac farewell tours
b) the amount of money Washington spent while you were reading this
c) the number of *Die Hard* sequels
d) (so far)

Actually, the correct answer is 'all four.' But that mammoth number also reoccurs in the realm of online social media. For example, Yahoo just coughed up $1.1 billion to buy a misspelled website named "Tumblr." (*Why* anybody would want to own a company that can't even spell synonyms for "breakfast cup," we don't know, but I suppose that's what you'd expect from a bunch of yahoos.)

Elsewhere online, latest estimates for online phenom, facebook, put its user community at over 1.1 billion, including as many as six people who listed their real age.

Over a billion people, all generating smiley faces and misspelling "tumbler." One of every seven people on the planet, all desperately hoping to be "liked," using the time-tested strategy of detailing their dinner plans, and re-sharing captioned pictures of a surly cat.

Think about that number. More than a billion of you. Why, if just 50% of you would promise to buy *just one* of my books, you'd be lying.

It's a staggering number. In fact, if facebook were a country with a population of 1.1 billion, it would be one of the five largest countries on Earth: Eric Holder would be arming their drug lords, and Ron Paul would be demanding we get our troops out of facebook.

Over a billion users. To give you some perspective, compare that to the number of Twitter users (500 million), or Pinterest (48 million), or Obama's healthcare exchange website (2).

But like any other collective hive-like organism that feeds on human insecurities, it's time for facebook to evolve. If you're listening, out there at facebook HQ, we need some stuff.

Here's an example of the problem: recently, a facebook friend posted that he'd been bitten by a spider. And *his* facebook friends kept clicking the "Like" button. Why? *Because they had nothing else to click* -- and heaven forbid they should just stay quiet for a bloody moment. But some people just can't stay quiet. Some people just can't not click, something...anything.

(Of course, we can't rule out the possibility that my friend just knows some seriously sick, pro-spider-venom-type individuals. I guarantee you that, somewhere on facebook, there's a page for transgendered arachnid-fetishist vegetarian vampires.)

But ever since facebook was about two days old, users have been clamoring for some new buttons; users who feel that it's time to look beyond the "Like" and deal with a broader range of emotions and opinions.

And I've come up with my own list of necessary emotions and opinions, which will not surprise anyone who's ever dated me.

It is, I think, an exceptional list, with some real typing time-savers, too. In addition to that single, limiting "Like" button, how about these new options:

~-~-~-~-~-~

- Don't like
- Seriously don't like
- You really need to get a life
- Liked at first, but the more I think about it...
- Half-like (the post is fine - it's you I can do without)
- Oh, now that's just nasty
- Would you please shut up already about the hotel you're checking into?

- Obviously, you're a pain troll who has nothing better to do than cause trouble
- Thanks for sharing that picture of you and your 4-H Club grand champion Angus steer, there at the Greater Chest Lesion County Fair And Turnip Festival
- If you send me one more invite to play "Candy Crush Saga," I will find you and hurt you
- You're posting a picture of you staring at yourself in the bathroom mirror of your own house? Seriously, darling? Could we get just a tiny bit more insecure there, Annie Hall?
- You know, when you decide to challenge my intelligence, it loses a bit of its sting when you type "your stupid"
- Sorry to challenge your pathos, but that "precious puppy" story was *not*, in fact, the most heartwarming thing I ever read in my whole life
- My goldfish has a better grasp of the English language than you
- So glad to hear that you're "on the way to the beach woo woo" -- I'm sure the several hundred million house burglars monitoring facebook are glad to hear it, too
- Yes, dear, we've all seen the grumpy cat meme
- That's the dumbest thing you've ever said since the last dumbest thing you ever said
- Yeah, nitey nite to you, too, Madwoman of Shallow

~-~-~-~-~-~

I've also discovered and described a new facebook syndrome, which, if we've ever dated, will not surprise you.

Meet the postjack. If you've spent more than ten minutes on facebook, you'll recognize the symptoms.

A postjack occurs when someone posts something topical, but then someone replies with something completely irrelevant to the original topic, and other people pick up the new topic, and soon the original topic has been spirited away to live with short-attention-span gypsies on a windswept scarp in a totally different conversation.

Here's a sample facebook conversation. (Yes, facebook conversations often are this insipid. Yes, it *is* kinda frightening.)

See if you can spot the postjack:

~-~-~-~-~-~

[Biff] I'm about to have some soup. Yum.

[Skeeterz Mom] I made soup last week. It was great lol.

[fb robot] MoleFungus wants you to play Candy Crush Saga!

[Agnes46] What kind of soup, Skeeter Mom?

[Choir Alto] You made soup and didn't bring me any? LOL

[Dwarf Cave Bat] I sometimes eat bread.

[Hot15] Bread! I'm like all yo and stuff. LOL!!!!!!!!!!!!!!!

[Agnes46] What kind of bread, Mr. Bat?

[Extremely Lonely Person] likes A1 steak sauce

[Biff] I heart bread lol

[fb robot] MoleFungus wants you to play Ultimate Zombie Solitaire!

[Skeeterz Mom] I like bread to.

[Disgruntled_Postal_Worker] I tell u what I dont like is peeps who talk during the movie

[fb robot] Dwarf Cave Bat likes this post

[Hot15] Amen LOL!!!!!!!!!!!

[fb robot] MoleFungus wants you to play Farmville Pioneer Mafia Holocaust!

[Dwarf Cave Bat] except raisin bread

[Disgruntled_Postal_Worker] u just wanna strangle em and its dark to in their

[Skeeterz Mom] omg

[Choir Alto] u2? I hate that! }: p

[Hot15] LOL!!!!!!!!

[Biff] I forgot what I was gonna eat rotflmao

[fb robot] MoleFungus wants you to play Manhattan Toxic Chemical Spill!

[Extremely Lonely Person] Here's a picture of my steak sauce

~-~-~-~-~-~

Insidious, ain't it? So don't do it, people! Fight it! Stay on topic! Don't succumb to postjacking!

And watch out for spiders. LOL.

Death by a Thousand Glitches

Vaporware, government style

<>~<>~~~~~~~~~~<>~<>~~~~~~~~~~<>~<>

[click]

"Okay, let's check this bad boy out."

[wait]

[click] [click]

Welcome to the ObamaCare website! Please wait...

[wait]

Welcome to the ObamaCare website! Thank you for w

[wait]

"What th..."

[click click click click click]

====================
We're sorry. The ObamaCare website is down.
[US GOV GLITCH 6f39-4B29-991b]
====================

"Whoa. This could take a while."

[refresh]

Welcome back to the ObamaCare website! We notice your subscriptions have changed since your last visit. Please click 'Confirm Changes' to continue.

"My *what*? *What* subscriptions?"

[click] [wait]

We are currently experiencing extremely minor glitches, since this site was designed to handle, like, four visitors at a time. Please wait, and whatever you do, don't hit your browser's Back button...

['Back' button click] [wait]

We seem to be having an extremely minor glitch locating your ObamaCare account. This could have been caused by clicking your browser's Back button. Or not. As if *we* knew. Please wait while we generate another error message.

[click] [wait]

The System is down at the moment. Please try again later. If you wish to contact us by phone for support, please dial 1-800-LAME-WEB, but not right now, as we are experiencing higher than normal call volume due to extremely minor glitches. When calling, please refer to the 428-character error code at the bottom of this screen, which, due to an extremely minor glitch, will vanish in about 10 seconds.

['Next' button click]

I'm sorry. First Name is a required flied.

"*Flied*? Are you kidding me? Required ***flied***???"

Don't get snippy, citizen.

"Okay. First name. B-o-b."

[click] [wait]

???ffe.ee.myAccount.login.header???

???ffe.ee.myAccount.login.username???

???ffe.ee.myAccount.login.trouble???

"What th..."

[refresh] [wait]

Thank you for w

[wait]

[click click click click click]

====================

We're sorry. The ObamaCare website is down.
[US GOV GLITCH B776-4K05-806c]

====================

"Oh, for the love of..."

['Google search results' click]

Welcome to the ObamaCare website! Please wait...

[wait]

Welcome back, Laura!

"*Laura?* But my name is Bob!"

Our records show that your name is Laura. Told you not to hit that 'Back' button.

"How do I update my name in your database to Bob?"

Hey, pal. You wouldn't believe the unholy mess in here. Believe me - it'll be easier on everybody if you just change your name to Laura.

"Sigh."

Did you just say 'sigh?'

[click click click click click]

Thank you, Lau

[wait]

[click click click click click]

====================
We're sorry. The ObamaCare website is down.
[US GOV GLITCH 0f2F-41F5-B96m]
====================

[click click click click click]

[wait]

Welcome back, Porfirio! To continue to finish, please select your State from the States dropdown list, which for some moronic reason includes Guam and the Northern Mariana Islands.

[click]

We're sorry, but ObamaCare is not currently available in the Northern Mariana Islands. Don't get cute, Porfirio.

[click] [wait]

Thank you. To continue, please answer the following questions. You'd be well advised to answer as truthfully as possible; after all, we didn't hire 16,000 additional IRS agents for nothing.

Do you speak Spanish?

a) No
b) Si
c) Que?

For security reasons, please enter

a) the hometown of the mother of your favorite teacher's first pet
b) that 428-character code from earlier
c) pi

The primary reason I'm signing up for ObamaCare is

a) to secure healthcare coverage for my spouse's pre-existing condition
b) to stay out of prison
c) to experience the unbridled joy, now that we finally got rid of the kids, of having them move back in with us until they turn 26, or I kill myself, whichever comes first

For whom are you looking for health care for?

a) Me
b) My family
c) I just want to pitch in and help out the idiot that wrote this question

Have you or any of your dependents ever had

a) persistent bleeding
b) lingering death
c) opposable thumbs

Question Placeholder (*remove after website has been tested*)

a) Lorem ipsum dolor sit amet
b) Lorem ipsum dolor sit amet
c) Lorem ipsum dolor sit amet

From the following list of options, please select the most amazing leader in the history of the Universe:

a) Barack Obama

Based on everything I've heard about government-run universal health care coverage, I expect to pay

a) less than I was paying before
b) a fair market price
c) out the batootie

You and your family may qualify for discount healthcare vouchers, based on several factors that we're pretty sure we wrote down on a cocktail napkin during "Binge Web Development Night" at Hooters. As far as we can recall, you might qualify for a discount if:

a) you live in another country
b) you live in South Florida and wear black socks with sandals (that one *still* cracks us up)
c) you are immeasurably vain and your last name rhymes with "snow comma"

Thanks to ObamaCare, I will now be able to

a) get a free pregnancy test, even though I'm a 57-year-old male
b) hemorrhage to death while waiting for a web page to load
c) have my spleen removed by an accountant

~-~-~-~-~-~

Porfirio, you're almost done with the initial sign-up phase! Please click 'Finish' to continue.

"Click 'finish' to continue, eh? Brilliant. What next - click 'Start' to finish?"

[click]

Porfirio, you're practically ready to begin the process of choosing your personalized secret questions, and then you'll be almost nearly ready to actually log in! Just one more qu

[wait]

[click]

[wait]

"Oh, I am *not* believing this."

[click] [click] [click] [click] [fist-click] [fist-click]

===================

We're sorry.
The ObamaCare website is down for scheduled maintenance.
===================

"Nooooooooooooo!"

Black Eye Friday

"Deck them all and grab their holly..."

<>~<>~~~~~~~~~~<>~<>~~~~~~~~~~<>~<>

Black Friday 2013. It was historic. America retail outlets set several new "day after Thanksgiving" records ... total shoppers, items sold, firearms discharged.

By the time the stores finally closed on Black Friday - if they actually closed at all - cost-savvy American shoppers had spent over $12 billion, on all the traditional holiday items: toys and dolls, deeply-discounted flat-screen TVs, and personal injury lawyers.

By now, thanks to smartphone cameras and in-store security systems, I'm sure you've seen some of the seasonal good cheer, festive fisticuffs, and bared-fang greed on display during Black Friday. People clawing over other people, neighbors shoving neighbors to the floor, face-offs between frighteningly plus-sized women armed with handbags the size of airplane hangars.

At one Walmart, shoppers were acting less like shoppers, and more people during the 1975 evacuation of Saigon, except the people in Saigon were better behaved.

And better dressed.

Watching some of the videos, it was hard to believe that these were really just stores - the same stores that were there yesterday, and would be here tomorrow. This wild-eyed hysteria could've easily been mistaken for a scene from the 70's, those few seconds after the arena doors are unlocked at a rock concert, but instead of a shrieking torrent of underfed coeds in bell-bottoms, it was everybody's Mother.

But this year, things went beyond the normal, jolly, holiday trampling and the joyous seasonal eye-gouging. This year, the biggest Black Friday decision at the big box stores was where the Salvation Army should set up their collection kettles -- inside or outside the yellow-taped 'crime scene' cordons.

At a store in Philly, a woman got in a fight with another shopper over an item they both wanted. Badly. So, channeling the giving spirit of Saint Nicholas, she zapped the other shopper with a stun gun.

"Oh, you better watch out..."

Somewhere in Virginia, a fight broke out between two guys over a parking space. One of the men graciously surrendered the spot, though, after the other guy stabbed him.

"You better not cry..."

During one live in-store segment from Toys 'R' Us in Times Square, the reporter actually said, out loud, that there was no violence *at this time.*

"You better not pout, or I'll punch out your eye..."

Some of the insanity can be attributed to businesses beginning Black Friday a bit earlier than usual...like, say, March. As each chain store jockeyed to out-early everybody else, crowds were teased to get start shopping earlier and earlier: at dawn Friday; then midnight Thursday; then 9pm; 6pm; 4pm; in utero. I'm surprised stores didn't install warming trays in their shopping carts, so shoppers could simply bring their Thanksgiving dinner with them and eat it while walking the crowded aisles.

And the crowds came. By the time Macy's in New York City opened its doors at 8pm on Thanksgiving Day, there were 15,000 people clustered outside waiting to get inside. Fifteen thousand people. Why, that's 14,994 more people than were able to use Obama's HealthScare.gov website on the day it almost nearly sort of started partly working.

(Actually, we don't know if Obama voters drove out and bought things, or if they just sat home waiting for people to bring them stuff.)

Nor did Black Friday end on Black Friday. Witness:

Hurry! Black Friday Savings End Sunday!

VISA did its part to helped spur the spending spirit by issuing a trendy new Black Card, the ultimate "look at me" status symbol, a card with a yearly fee of $500 and who knows what credit limit...if any. This kind of showy desperation is the fuel that feeds Jaguar dealerships everywhere; it's what talk show hosts call a "middle-age crisis" or, as psychologists would put it, "compensation."

Despite the Black Wednesday-Thru-Sunday Friday frenzy, though, stock prices for the big box stores took a bit of a hit in November, dropping overall by 2%. Analysts quickly pointed out all the seasonal costs of cleaning up blood stains and patching up bullet holes.

By the way, when it's time to mail those Christmas cards, you'll be happy to hear that we have a new batch of holiday stamps from the US Post Office, that paragon of taut fiscal efficiency. This year, they've released these religiously-respectful favorites:

- a menorah stamp, for those celebrating Hanukkah
- a kinara stamp, for those celebrating Kwanzaa
- a gingerbread house stamp, for those celebrating, uh, processed sugar

But now I need to run. I have to gird up for Cyber Warfare Monday, which started last Saturday. In the spirit of the season, I'll leave you with this touching anecdote:

Thanksgiving evening, one family I know decided to take advantage of the special deals being advertised for Black It Ain't Even Friday Yet Friday, and so at 9pm they bundled up and headed out. At their first stop, a cavernous clothing outlet named Old Grizzled Navy Guy, in-store crowds had already pegged the local fire department's occupancy limits, so bitter, frigid store clerks had to stand outside with bitter, frigid discount-hunter-gatherers, letting the savages in only as sated shoppers exited.

This thing had "Lord of the Flies" written all over it...

My friend and his wife decided to divide and conquer; their thinking, apparently, being that if they hit two stores at once, they could experience much more suffering. He left his wife to stick it out at the Navy place, while he went next door to Home Target Depot Lobby Mart, a store so large that even Bruce Willis couldn't blow it up.

Of course, the crowds were just as gigantic at Home Target Depot Lobby Mart. And just as polite, too, in a flesh-eating pre-civilization kind of way.

Anyway, nearly two hours later my friend hooked back up with his wife, who was still numbly waiting outside Old Grizzled Navy Guy. My friend made an ill-advised joke, ducked judiciously, and then spelled his wife in the grumbling line, so she could go buy a divorce.

And that's how I got to hear the story. I had to go pick him up at the Navy Guy store.

See, in the settlement, she got the car.

You Too Can Be Non-Essential!

Wasn't this supposed to suck?

<>~<>~~~~~~~~~~<>~<>~~~~~~~~~~<>~<>

If there's one thing we've all learned from the government shutdown of 2013, it's this: the best ... um ... no, wait, the worst ... uh ... hang on ... never mind. We didn't learn *anything* from the shutdown. Cause the shutdown didn't *do* anything.

But it sure was fun to not watch while it wasn't happening.

Much like its ten-month-older sibling of doom, the dreaded (*gasp*) Sequester (*aaaiiieee!*), this shutdown thing has been all ado about nothing...except for the political Jeremiahs selling the dread. In fact, the only *real* damage done during sequestration was to unobservant people who got trampled because they happened to be standing between a member of Congress and a microphone.

Remember the year 2000? The apocalyptic Y2K scare? Deep-eyed, somber stormcrows prophesied that all the world's financial markets would collapse at midnight, as if global commerce were Cinderella's pumpkin. Mankind's fragile social fabric was doomed to dissolve into chaos! Why, the evening news might start before (*or after!*) 6 pm; fast-food restaurants would just randomly refuse to Biggie-Size; mynah birds would suddenly develop Tourette's ... all because nobody had ever thought to build a computer that could add 1,999 plus 1.

And then...nothing happened. The year 2000 rolled right on in, and nothing happened, except for Congress passing a much-needed law that banned anyone from ever again playing the Prince tune *1999*.

But compared to all the failed predictions of disaster, this year's government shutdown made Y2K look like the middle reel of *Independence Day*. This current shutdown has been like a Kardashian: much noise, but there's not really anything there.

What we did get to see, though, was a lot of petty political parlor tricks, and some staggering stupidity. I mean, even by *Washington* standards, it was staggering. And pockets of irony so thick they showed up on weather charts. Witness:

~-~-~-~-~-~

The mainstream media were quick to grasp the salient, democracy-threatening elements of the budget battle, as crackerjack investigative reporters broke the story that, at the zoo in DC, there was no money to run the panda-cam.

~-~-~-~-~-~

Republicans ran about town, yelling, "Look, you. Give us what we want, or the government gets it, see?" Democrats ran about town, yelling, "Look, you. Give us what we want, or the government gets it, see?"

See the obvious, deeply-seated ideological differences?

Naturally, the mainstream media took sides, as any professional, wholly objective observer of events would do. The media immediately blamed a group of conservatives who call themselves the Tea Party - a Volkswagen van-sized clutch of non-violent citizens who, despite making up *less than ten percent of the minority party*, are apparently viewed by the mainstream media as immortal thunderbolt-wielding shape-shifters from hell.

~-~-~-~-~-~

After a week of all this society-crippling shutdown - we think it was a week...it was hard to tell - Congress bravely decided to work during part of the weekend to get things resolved.

Go figure. The only time we can get the government to actually show up for work is when the government is closed.

~-~-~-~-~-~

At one point during the "negotiations" to re-open the government, President Tee Time set up his own bipartisan meeting between the major players in Congress. But then he trotted out little Jay-Jay Carney, his fourteen-year-old press mouthpiece, to announce that the President would not budge on his demands. In other words, there would be no negotiating at the negotiation.

Hey. Don't say I didn't warn you. This is a special kind of stupid.

~-~-~-~-~-~

Amidst all the other madness, an ex-dental assistant suddenly decided to take on the Secret Service and the entire Capitol police department, armed with nothing but her car. Afterwards, we learned that the car-blitzer was convinced that President Tee Time had been speaking to her via secret radio waves. No word on whether the President was willing to psychically negotiate.

~-~-~-~-~-~

Of course, it was just a matter of time before blame-lobbing members of Congress bit into *that* story. Texas Representative Sheila Jackson-Hole, who always look like she's wearing an overcooked radial tire on her head, lashed herself to a microphone on the House floor and starting cataloging government shutdown victims, including the Lindbergh baby, Beethoven's hearing, both Cain *and* Abel, and an extinct Jurassic oyster fungus that claimed to be Hairy Screed's college roommate.

Despite several attempts by the Capitol police to get her to "yield back her time," including tranquilizer darts, Jackson-Hole ranted and waved her arms around until a nearby sentence finally had enough and committed suicide by leaping out of her mouth.

"Piecemeal is undeserving of America," she pointed out.

Well, what're you gonna do? It's hard to argue with rock-solid logical oratory like that.

After the poor sentence had been laid to rest, Jackson-Hole was asked why she brought up the crazed woman driver in DC in the context of the government shutdown.

"Because I have First Amendment rights," she replied, possibly in response to some question from an entirely different conversation.

Ah. Thanks, Big Hat. We'll eagerly await your laser-focused, highly relevant budget-based discussion of zebras, mood rings, and ear wax.

~-~-~-~-~-~

In a possibly related story: somewhere on the National Mall, a man set himself on fire. He died - as often happens to people who douse themselves with flammable materials - but not before being fined by Capitol police for self-immolation without a permit during a government shutdown.

~-~-~-~-~-~

As part of a typically spastic effort to remain relevant, former House Speaker Nancy Neurosi sent a letter to the current House Speaker. Inside sources say it was the letter "E."

In lighter news, ex-Speaker Nancy's tired, trademark necklace took first runner-up in Delaware's annual Wilma Flintstone Look-Alike contest.

~-~-~-~-~-~

One interview, I only heard on my car radio, so I have to paraphrase. But I think I'm pretty close:

Liberal pol: People are hurting! It breaks my *heart*! We *have* to compromise!
Reporter: So the Democrats are ready to compromise?
Lib: No.

~-~-~-~-~-~

When interviewed about the "negotiations," Senate Leader Hairy Screed issued these memorable, monument-worthy words: "The President of the United States was very strong, strong, strong."

After the press conference, Hairy dashed away to his next Leader of the entire United States Senate appointment, where he switched into an "I Heart Obama" spandex jumpsuit and paraded back and forth in the Rose Garden, humming six-note snippets of Al Green tunes.

~-~-~-~-~-~

Maryland's Representative Steny "Lockjaw" Hoyer and his teeth postured that he sure wished politicians would quit holding all these press conferences.

He said it at a press conference.

Hoyer's teeth could not be reached for comment, and the Department of Homeland Security knows why, and I hope some of you will appreciate just how complex that joke really was.

~-~-~-~-~-~

Given the madness, it was really no surprise to see President Tee Time's popularity drop to 40%. In fact, what's maybe *harder* to believe is that 4 of 10 people *still* think the guy is doing a good job.

Ponder that, America. Next time you're in the checkout line at the grocery, pick out ten random people. (they'll all be standing in front of you anyway, in the Express Lane, acting like they never in their dim lives wrote a check before)

Statistically, four of those people think President Tee Time is knockin' it out of the park.

Now, the fun part: take note of what's in their grocery baskets. I'm thinking free range tuna, milk from some plant (almond, soy, Hairy Screed), and a discreetly-tinted tube of that "how to hide scars" gel.

And these people vote. Sometimes twice.

~-~-~-~-~-~

Nor was the private sector immune to the lure of the madness. Men's clothier Jos. A Bank issued a new ad: Buy one suit at the regular price, or the Tea Party will shut down the government.

~-~-~-~-~-~

Finally, here's what may be the single stupidest pronouncement since Eve said, "Honey? Taste this."

The White House announced that, because of that big ole, mean, naughty shutdown, they weren't going to be able to afford keeping up The First Michelle's account at Twitter.

I know, I know...Twitter is free. I know that, you know that, my neighbor's five-year-old knows that. But somehow the White House doesn't know that. Apparently, they read about as much of the Twitter bylaws as they read of ObamaCare.

Of course, you understand the implications: the Federal government has finally figured out how to run out of money paying for something that's free.

Ah, The Noise of Home Ownership

Like it nearly, sorta, kinda, almost never even happened.

<>~<>~~~~~~~~~~<>~<>~~~~~~~~~~<>~<>

I knew something was wrong when I saw water on the kitchen floor.

Yeah, I'm quick like that.

WEDNESDAY :: ~6.30p

I was working from home, wrapping up another fulfilling day of writing enough software to ensure that my little charge of corporate Americans could keep making their boat payments.

I got up, to change the music and to restock the ice chilling my Coke Zero, and saw the water. Lightning-like thinker that I am, I sensed a problem.

Let's cut to the chase: the pipe feeding my bathroom faucet had popped loose. By the time I visited the crime scene, the floor was nearly an inch under water. My "master" bathroom had become a candidate for a 1940s water ballet, assuming the stars were Danny DeVito and Barbara Mikulski. And the rest of the impatient water had soaked its way through my carpeted bedroom, found *that* boring, and decided to tour the kitchen.

I won't psychically scar you by describing the nauseating sound a waterlogged bedroom carpet makes under bare feet.

WEDNESDAY :: ~6.32p

Initially, I just stood there, an idiot in the water, like some lobotomized cypress knee. I just stood there, staring at the standing inch of uninvited water in my bathroom. Finally, it occurred to me that I own towels.

I'm quick like that.

WEDNESDAY :: ~8.00p

Around 8:00p, I had emptied the cement pond into the tub ... towel by towel by hand-wrung towel. "Well done," I thought. "Well done."

Then I remembered the carpet in the bedroom.

WEDNESDAY :: ~8.02p

Every sea-lab footprint across my Fortress of Solitude, from the bathroom doorway to the kitchen doorway, was a blurry Sasquatch wet-cast. As a test, I planted a foot and watched...watched as water pooled, around my foot, from in and under the bedroom carpet.

And I have to say, at the risk of causing a metaphor collision, that's when it sank in:

This event is bigger than me.

I called the insurance.

WEDNESDAY :: ~8.30p

I fully expected to get an after-hours recording, at which point I would do what any man would do: entertain a few semi-violent thoughts about the insurance agent, quietly insult his genetic heritage and choice of social partners, and then head for the spare bedroom for tossage and turnage.

But the insurance answered the phone. An actual human being answered the phone.

Next, I expected the standard full-bore Insurance Company denial dance:

- The number you have dialed is not a valid integer
- I'm sorry, Mr. Valued Client, but your alleged flood damage occurred with six statute miles of a non-binding vernal equinox, and sadly that's not covered under your Submariner Druid Exclusion Rider, Section Five-Oh-Five-Zed.
- Que?

But no. The insurance said they'd take care of everything.

Things were looking up at Cement Pond Central.

WEDNESDAY :: ~8.40p

Not only did I make contact with the insurance, but *they* contacted a disaster recovery company - I won't mention them by name, but it rhymes with Swerve-Crow - and I was promised a suck-up team (no the *other* suck-up) within the hour.

WEDNESDAY :: ~within the hour

As it turns out, Swerve-Crow has some very loud machines. But I'm getting ahead of myself. That part wouldn't happen till around midnight.

Before I became acquainted with the high-decibel industrial fans and two-story humidifiers, Swerve-Crow first carted in a cadre of green machines with long blue hoses. And those mastodon-trunked machines sucked on my bedroom carpet like IRS agents trying to get pocket money for their next Line Dancing & Drive-Thru Colonoscopy seminar.

The head Swerve-Crow was amazingly efficient. He supervised the drying stage, organized the fan placements, took copious notes and made twenty-seven million measurements of my home, using some kind of tape measure that seemed to actually levitate.

THURSDAY :: ~12.49a

Swerve-Crow and their aqua-suckers had done all they could do. They had parted my Bed Sea, and now it was time for the aforementioned very loud machines.. Nine fans, on loan from Dante's Seventh Level Gaping Maw Wind Tunnel Inc., and two anal-retentive dehumidifiers that could extract moisture from a mummy's navel.

I live two miles from the airport. When Swerve-Crow powered up this Army of Baskervilles, the runway lights dimmed.

And then it began. A loud, endless, endless thrumming. My house sounded like the carney side of a county fair.

And Team Swerve-Crow departed.

THURSDAY :: ~1.00a

But there's more adventure, more discovery. Over my years of home ownership, I'd been vaguely aware of an untraveled portion of my house known to normal people as the "guest bedroom." I remember the realtor had gone on about it while showing me the house. At the time, I hadn't paid much attention...I was busy calculating the distance from my future fridge to my future couch.

So, tonight - for the first time in my life - I'm sleeping in my guest bedroom. What's protocol? Should I turn down my quilt and leave a pillow chocolate? Should I expect breakfast, or provide breakfast? Or is this what my Jamaican friend used to call "Breakfast Jump Up" -- where *you* jump up and you make you *own* breakfast, you lazy ball head.

DAY TWO :: ~3.30p

Thinking ahead, I called a plumber, so he could repair the sink next week.

Somebody from the insurance came by; possibly he was the Claim Agent, or the Adjustor, or the Mitigator, or the Spanish Inquisition. Heck, for all I know, he was that sex offender who, according to the Official Sex Offender Registry, lives somewhere near me under a red dot. All I know is he had a business card and a business clipboard. And, of course, a gravity-defying tape measure. He explained many technical and legal things, though not to me, took copious notes, and ... measured ... again.

Then he gave me a brief idea of what to expect over the next days, and weeks, although it could take longer, so plan for that, and before he could complete that sentence, I hit him with the clipboard.

I called the plumber back to cancel. Next week, there won't even *be* a sink to fix yet.

NIGHT TWO :: ~8.00p

These fans are starting to get on my nerves.

The size of the Disruption Factor is beginning to kick in, too. For example, my kitchen is half-gutted. That includes linoleum, sub-flooring, and counter units that used to be attached to the walls.

For sups, I wanted to heat up a nice bowl of soup. I had to go out to the garage to get a pot. And a spoon.

And the soup.

DAY THREE :: ~2.30p

I left all the fans running and went to work, then spent the morning driving back home to make sure my house hadn't desiccated like some starved spider.

As scheduled, an optimistic, several-days-early-at-least contractor came by and ... measured. These disaster people need to work on their communication skills.

NIGHT THREE :: ~8.00p

Okay, as the bold headline already said, this is Night Three of playing host to a nonet of Swerve-Crow industrial fans. Mighty fine workers they are, these fans, but not much in the way of stimulating conversation. Just that one word is about it. That one looooooong word, over, and over, and over, and over again.

It was the sound one of Tolkien's Ents might make saying 'aah' for a Fangorn dentist.

That one, loud, continuous, somnolent, torpid word.

That. Loud. Endless. One-tone. Deafening. Dirge.

If you see me in the news, picking off coeds from a college bell tower with a Second Amendment-protected pop tart, you'll know why.

NIGHT FOUR :: ~11.59p

I hate them. These evil, foul-mouthed, one-note, shrieking Swerve-Crow fans. I hate them.

I have tickets to the Symphony, but I don't even want them anymore. Not tonight. The program is Wagner, and I don't need to drive into town to hear about the Valkyrie ... I'm *living* with the Valkyrie.

I'm ready to do something dark, violent, and heartless, like go find a bar that's having Open Mike Night, wait for the singer to begin, then leap to my feet and start screaming, "Derivative! That's so *derivative!*"

You know - it just occurred to me - I don't *have* to stay here in this jump up exurban *Twister* sound stage. I give up. I'm getting a hotel room.

Nearly a hundred moor-hound howling hours it took me, to figure that out.

I'm quick like that.

Rogue Rabbits & Renegade Money

There ought to be a law. Wait...there is.

<>~<>~~~~~~~~~~<>~<>~~~~~~~~~~<>~<>

America. We are a nation of laws, as we all learned from *Jeopardy* reruns or, occasionally, school.

"A nation of laws." This is a point of national pride for every American; at least, every American who has stuff worth stealing. Of course, for every stealee, there's a potential stealer. Yin and yang. After all, this is America - the land of opportunity. And *that* segment of the population - the Americans who steal stuff from the Americans who have stuff - they don't care much about a nation of laws. They're more drawn to the other America: a nation of lawyers.

And they're rarely disappointed.

Laws and lawyers. Yin and yang. Eggs and bacon. Sharks and chum.

And the laws may be losing. Trust me: right now, some enterprising guy is driving through your neighborhood (it's always a guy), trying to figure out how he can quietly rip out your copper plumbing while carjacking your SUV so he can boil it down for bulk resale, which is where we get the term "melting pot."

So just how many laws do you think there are in America? Well, according to one source on the internet (yeah, yeah, I know), there are (and I quote) "thousands if not more."

Uh, yeah.

Imagine the Leon Spinks' sparring partner who came up with *that* clever calculation. Better yet, imagine the meeting in which some humanoid group with questionable motor skills decided that *that* was the guy who should be spokesman.

The source continues (and I quote): "It hard to have exact number..."

Whoa. It hard to have doubting when source be's so much smart and stuff.

As it turns out, knowing exactly how many laws there are in America may be a calculation beyond our ken. To give you some scale: so far this year, according to the internet (yeah, yeah, I know), legislators have shoved some 30,000 new laws into the United States' collective penal code. (29,998 of them were just bills naming various high schools and post offices. The other two provided Congressional exemptions for investments in copper plumbing.)

Some have posited that we now have so many laws, *somebody's* breaking *some* law, right now, every second of every day. And most of those people are driving in front of me.

Here are a few of this year's new laws:

~-~-~-~-~-~

HR 475: To amend the Internal Revenue Code of 1986 to include vaccines against seasonal influenza within the definition of taxable vaccines.

Lovely. The IRS has figured out a way to tax the flu. Close call, though. They almost missed a microbe.

~-~-~-~-~-~

HR 1071: To specify the size of the precious-metal blanks that will be used in the production of the National Baseball Hall of Fame commemorative coins.

Go ahead. Admit it. You weren't aware that the size of those Cooperstown commemorative coins had gotten so out of control, were you?

Actually, this one's an amendment. Apparently, something slipped past the umpire in the original 2011 law, HR 2527, the National Baseball Hall of Fame Commemorative Coin Act, and Congress had to overreact quickly. Fortunately, we have alert, national security-focused members of Congress who grasp the potential peril of unregulated baseball memorabilia. Take *that*, radical global terrorism!

~-~-~-~-~-~

SB 3579 (Illinois): It is unlawful for a child sex offender to participate in a holiday event...wearing an Easter Bunny costume.

Seriously, Illinois? Has this become a problem?

Next thing you know, any giant egg-laying rabbit spotted in Chicago with flu symptoms and a handful of oversized coins will be executed on the spot.

~-~-~-~-~-~

So. This is what our State and Federal lawgivers have been up to. But how about some laws that address *real* problems? Here are some suggestions:

- If your internet service is down, it shall be unlawful during that downtime for your cable/internet provider to run television ads about their award-winning internet service.
- No longer may a rock band release a 'Greatest Hits' album that includes one song you can't get anywhere else even though you already bought all their other albums. (Additional fines may be levied against bands who have had more than ten Farewell Tours.)
- It shall be unlawful for a pharmaceutical company to push a drug that has more side-effects than benefits. At least 50% of the drug's TV commercial must

discuss something other than how the drug might kill you, your spouse, or your lawn. No 60-second spot may consist of 4 short seconds of bragging, followed by 56 seconds of muttered warnings, threats, and potential side-effects, including death and other, even nastier things that I will not mention here, other than to say that it rhymes with "spectral geekage."

- *AMENDMENT:* Drug companies may no longer refer to death as a "possible side-effect." Calling death a side-effect is like calling out-of-wedlock triplets a "dating hassle."
- For obvious reasons, NBC shall no longer be allowed to call its news division "the news division."
- In the state of Alabama, football team nicknames have gotten out of control, and the state's Capitol must stage an emergency mascot intervention. The Auburn University football team shall no longer be allowed to refer to themselves as the Tigers, *and* the War Eagles, *and* the Wordham Eagles. And the University of Alabama must pick a nickname and stick with it - they can't keep being the Crimson Tide, *and* the Crimson White, *and* have an elephant mascot named Al who refuses to wear pants.
- The following expressions are hereby banned from political discourse: *at the end of the day*, *when the rubber hits the road*, *let me be perfectly clear*, and *my distinguished colleague.* Additionally, any politician who ever says *as I've always said* will be subject to an immediate beheading. (not that *that* would stop them from talking...)

- Geraldo Rivera shall be reclassified as a toxic substance. Think DDT. Think chemical weapons. Think huge commemorative coins.
- Any time a driver lurches into your lane while texting, you shall have the right to travel back in time and neuter the driver's parents.
- Bill O'Reilly, host of the wildly popular *O'Reilly Factor*, may now interrupt a maximum of 45 guests per hour. Fines will be levied on a graduated scale, up to and including the host having to appear in public wearing an off-the-rack suit.
- When you're shopping for a new jacket and you ask if the jacket is waterproof, it shall be unlawful for the salesperson to duck your question with a perky, "Well, it's water-resistant!" Water-resistant is *not* the same thing as water-proof. Heck, I'm *death*-resistant.

And speaking of shopping -- ever been in town and found yourself in the middle of an armed robbery? At least, it sure *feels* like a robbery, and you're definitely being physically attacked by a stranger -- but as you pose for a quick selfie, you're not exactly sure what to say in your status update on facebook. Felony? Misdemeanor? Aggravated? OMG LOL?

There's an app for that.

If you've an iPhone and a spare $5.99, you can download the entire New York State Penal Code. It'll come in handy on those more hectic crime-fighting days.

After all, somebody's gotta ride herd on those rabbits.

Shirley He's Not Syria's

It's sad when the news is funnier than the funnies

<>~<>~~~~~~~~~~<>~<>~~~~~~~~~~<>~<>

[fade bumper music, cut to studio, CAM 1]

Welcome back, folks. I'm Tawny Molars, and thanks for joining us for this special edition of *Handbasket on Hell's Highway*, the top-rated eye-on-American-events morning show! We've got lots of hard news to cover this morning - earth-shaping events, like the escalating situation in Syria; more problems with the HealthCare bill; who should play Batman - but first, let's have another look at that awful Miley Cyrus video.

[roll film]

Folks, we'll be right back after several minutes of car commercials featuring loud salesmen standing in windy parking lots.

[roll commercial]

Welcome back, folks. I'm Holder Spillet, in for Tawny Molars. Leading our news this morning is Syria, and an announcement by the White House that the President is expected to make a statement announcing his tentative plans to announce a possible meeting designed to formalize tentative potential options for no longer postponing the de-classification of intelligence that would clear the way for a good chance of tentatively planning to announce a planning meeting.

Ladies and gentlemen, *that* is good stuff. They don't call it "the most transparent administration in history" for nothin'.

Just minutes from now, we'll be going live to a press event with the Secretary of State. Say! While we wait, let's get a weather update from Biff Colongard, who, as usual, is standing outside eating some sponsor's free food while participating in a Lowe's Depot home repair segment and greeting a hand bell choir from some barefoot burg in central Kansas. But first, let's take another look at that horrible Miley Cyrus video.

[roll film]

Folks, we're looking now at live pictures of an empty podium somewhere in the White House. Any minute now, we're expecting to hear from the Secretary of State, who we're told has been working hard at developing an entirely new emotion. This would be, I believe, his second. Have I got those numbers right, Biff?

[cut to exterior, REM 4]

Hi, Tawny! You are corre...

[off-camera mic] Biff, it's me, Holder.

Sorry. Hi, Holder! You are correct. The Secretary of State is well-known for his numb stare, basset-hound pout, and corpse-like enthusiasm. According to one source, he looks like a badly-handled hat tree that somebody painted a face on.

[off-camera mic] Thanks, Biff. How're things looking, weather-wise, using our exclusive Super-Maxi Quantum-Color Robo-Doppler Sky-Cluster All-4-U Instalert Radar?

As you know, Holder, it's been such a busy storm season that we're running out of names. Right now, we're keeping an eye on Tropical Depression 493, which at any moment could become Hurricane Millard Fillmore. If there's any wind-whipped carnage, we'll let you know! Back to you, Tawny.

[off-camera mic] *Holder.*

Sorry.

[cut to studio, CAM 1]

Thanks, Biff. Folks, we've just learned that the President is running a bit behind schedule; he was leaving the Oval to start another war when he tripped over his Nobel Peace Price. So let's take a quick break for some commercials featuring an imaginary bear family who are obsessed with toilet paper.

[roll commercial]

Welcome back to *Handbasket on Hell's Highway*! Right now, let's go live to the Secretary of State.

[cut to White House, podium one-shot, REM 11]

Hello, everybody. I'm the new Secretary of State that's not Hillary Clinton. Concerning the developing situation in Syria, I can assure the American public that the President has been focusing all his attention on the crisis, in-between tee times. We've spent the last several days consulting with our top military advisors, and we've burned much midnight oil, laboring over intense sessions of *Battleship* and a particularly enlightening game of *Risk*. Ultimately, of course, America's role in these heady world events will be decided by the President's wife. But as of right now, here's what I can tell you about our strategy:

It will not be boots on the ground.
It will not make a single sound.
It will not take a lot of time.
It will not cost a single dime.

We know they're there! We know we're here!
We know they know we know no fear!
We know *this* thing! We know *that* thing!
We know our President can sing!

[cut to studio, CAM 1]

That was the Secretary of State, clearly expressing up to two separate emotions while insisting he's not Hillary Clinton. And speaking of people who aren't Hillary Clinton, let's rerun that disgusting Miley Cyrus video.

[roll film]

Welcome back, folks! Right now, we're going live to a table, somewhere...possibly in the White House...where the President, the Vice President, and some visiting foreign dignitaries in unbelievably bad suits are looking appropriately thoughtful.

[cut to White House, possibly, REM 28]

Prez: Welcome, everybody. Folks, as I've always said, let me be perfectly clear. And now I'll take a few seemingly random questions. Yes, over there.

Reporter: Sir, in light of th...

Veep: *Hey!* First, state your @*#%^$ name and your newspaper.

Prez: Hold it down over there, Teeth Boy.

Veep: Sorry, big guy.

Reporter: Sir, I'm Ahmal Ovrett from the Baghdad Sentinel Tribune Gazette and D-Lux Coupon Clipper. What are America's battle plans?

Prez: Let me be perfectly clear. On the naval front, I've moved five warships into a tight, vulnerable non-maneuverable knot in the Eastern Mediterranean, as I've always said. I can get you the exact coordinates.

Joint Chief: Six.

Prez: Huh?

Joint Chief: Six warships. Six.

Prez: Five, six, whatever.

Reporter: B-9!

Veep: Hit!

Prez: You sunk my battleship!

Foreign Dignitaries: HA HA HA HA HA HA

Reporter in the back: Sir, is it true that you got your teleprompter speeches confused and granted Syria a HealthCare waiver but bombed the AFL-CIO?

Prez: Who let FoxNews in here?

Veep: I got this.

[*thwack*]

Ahmal: Sir, where again are the bombs targeted?

Prez: At 6:15 local time, we're taking out three non-union sandal factories on two streets in suburban Daalaabaalaalaa al q'aalude-isbad. Obviously, we can't divulge details. I mean, we're not stupid. So here's the...uh...the atitude-lay and the ongitude-lay.

Ahmal: If you would, please, here, on this map? Just here? And here? Yes?

Prez: Yeppers.

Ahmal: Do you have a phone I could use?

Prez: Here...have a free cellphone.

Ahmal: But I'm not a US citizen!

Prez: Whatever.

Another Reporter: Mr. President, would you care to comment on the sordid Miley Cyrus video?

Prez: If I had a son, he would look like Miley Cyrus.

Reporter: Have you personally seen the sleazy Miley Cyrus video?

Prez: No, but I intend to pivot like a laser and give the matter my full attention.

Bill Clinton: I got this.

Prez: Thanks, everybody. And now, I'd like to welcome my distinguished guests: these three irrelevant chair-fillers from the Baltic, who will sit here while I nod thoughtfully and make little up-and-down pointy shapes with my thumb and forefinger.

Baltic guest: We thought you were taller.

Prez: Whatever.

[cut to studio, CAM 1]

Welcome back, folks! Well, wasn't *that* a yawner? In case you missed it, either we just heard from the President, or else we piggybacked a promo feed from Madame Tussauds. Sheesh. The last time I saw a performance that wooden was in *Pinocchio.* I mean, the President was so lethargic, he made the Secretary of State look like Robin Williams on a meth binge.

And now, it's time for a quick commercial break, featuring mail-order diets that turn unattractive fat women into unattractive thin women, and shaving gels that turn ordinary men into Olympian lust magnets.

But first, let's have another look at that vile Miley Cyrus video!

Nobby and The Sap

Ever wanted to punch a song in the mouth?

<>~<>~~~~~~~~~~<>~<>~~~~~~~~~~<>~<>

Have you heard it? That bone-warping misery-fest masquerading as a song called *The Christmas Shoes*? A song so unbelievably soppy, so intentionally saccharine, it comes with an anti-depressant scrip.

This may be the first song in human history that can actually raise LDL cholesterol.

Or, even worse, have you seen it? There's an accompanying music video on YouTube...but of course there is. There's a video of everything on YouTube, including handwriting found on Mars, promises kept by the Obama administration, and other imaginary events.

How wretched is *The Christmas Shoes*? Here are some online reviews:

- most annoying song ever
- manipulative and worth missing

- I commented on you tube on how rediculously bad that song was and i got hate mail from a few religeous freaks wishing me death, lol

(Well, Commenter Number Three, if the "religeous freaks" don't whack you, your second-grade English teacher surely will, lol omg ups pdf asap)

The Christmas Shoes. It's the worst of those irritating, heartstring-tugging holiday concoctions, designed for no other reason than to make stagnant female facebook addicts weep, click 'Like,' type a misspelled comment with twelve exclamation points, and then 'Share' the foul thing with everybody else, along with tired, overused, obligatory comments like "U MUST C" and "cried my eyes out LOL."

In case you've lived a charmed life and missed this maudlin multimedia tragedy, here's the short version: a little boy wants to buy shoes for his mom, but he can't afford them, so a guy in line behind him pays for the shoes.

So far, so good, right? A nice, tight, sweet story, that could never possibly happen in America, or Detroit. Especially during the group psychosis we call the holiday shopping season.

Anyway, that's the short version. It's when you get to the full-blown five-minute rendition that the pain begins.

The morose Charles-Dickens-on-painkillers ditty doesn't mention the kid's name, but I always think of him as 'Nobby.' He looks like a Nobby to me, with his knitted *Duck Dynasty* skull cap and eyes the size of filmmaker Michael Moore's trans-fat budget. And the sap in line behind him - the guy who ends up paying for Nobby's shoes - the way he throws money around, his name might've been Nancy Pelosi.

Except this guy used his own money.

The song deprives us of much-needed detail. We could infer that Nobby's mom is sick -- as she bloody well might well be, given that it's winter and the poor woman is barefoot. Another bit of circumstantial evidence: Nobby says she might meet Jesus tonight. But maybe Mommy's a Major League Baseball scout, prospecting Cubans.

Other clues about Mom's condition: Nobby is in a hurry and "Daddy said there's not much time." But we can't *know* that she's sick - Mom could've been picked up for assembling fertilizer-based bombs, and at the last minute the Governor rejected her stay of execution, and now she's about to go all Green Mile at Leavenworth.

And how about The Sap? We're supposed to *believe* this contrived bit, in which some frenzied guy is trying to get out of the mall on Christmas Eve without drop-kicking the twenty-ninth consecutive Goth-attired teen who bumped into him while texting -- but yet he has both extra money *and* patience?

Oh, please. Have *you* ever seen guys in full-blown-last-minute-Christmas-shopping mode? Picture it: first, young Nobby irritates everybody in line by glacially excavating nickels and pennies from his pockets. And then, after Nobby makes the discovery that women's shoes cost more than $1.28, he spins around, urchin-stares up at the stranger in line behind him, and organizes a little impromptu violin concerto.

"Gee, mister. My cow-sized eyes and I don't have enough money. What am I gonna do, mister?"
"Well, for a start, you're gonna be a cold-footed little no-shoe-buying chap. Push off, measles monkey."

Over the years, people much smarter (and funnier) than I have wrestled with the damaging effects of being subjected to this seasonal Bummer Generator. For instance, one guy's *Christmas Shoes* survival tips included this handy advice: should the song suddenly occupy your car radio, remember to tuck in your shoulder before leaping out of the car. (the tuck helps facilitate a smoother roll across the freeway)

Other *Christmas Shoes* victims recommend more radical remedies: self-maiming; eardrum-ectomies; avoiding any inbound radio waves by blocking them with a large object, like Canada, or Michael Moore. But though the melody is admittedly malodorous, I don't think it calls for anything as drastic as having to look at Michael Moore. I mean, it's not like the thing's being sung by Burl Ives. Being forced to listen to Burl Ives singing *Christmas Shoes* would elevate this fairly pedestrian crime to the level of felony public menace, and require some tit-for-tat retribution, like public stoning, or being forced to watch a Ben Stiller marathon.

Defenders of this drippy, shameless spectacle...and there are defenders, although both of them live in a severely-gated community named 'Happy Lawns' that has curfews, limited visitation, and lots of padding...will argue that *Christmas Shoes* is a touching depiction of what Christmas is all about.

I disagree.

Christmas is about music...specifically, Christmas music. And the definition of "Christmas music" is non-negotiable. When a candidate carol is attempting to qualify as Christmas music, certain things are immediate disqualifiers:

- any song that, like *Christmas Shoes*, makes you want to drive a bus into an overpass truss
- any song that begins in a minor key and then, contrary to every accepted form of musical decency in the known universe, ends in a major key
- Burl Ives

Besides, no self-respecting lyricist would pen this couplet:

I'll never forget the look on his face
When he said "Momma's gonna look so great."

Seriously. *Face*, he rhymes with *great*.

Good grief. No wonder she's shoeless.

While in Jersey, Visit Sunny Islamabad!

Bats, bananas, and bad PR

<>~<>~~~~~~~~~~<>~<>~~~~~~~~~~<>~<>

You have to wonder: what the heck did Newark do?

We're talking, of course, about this year's results from the coveted "Top Ten Friendliest Cities in America" poll...and its less pursued, wart-pocked evil step-sister, the "Most Unfriendly Cities" list. If you missed it, taking the dishonors in this year's step-sister list:

Newark, New Jersey.

It makes you wonder just who the judges met in Jersey. And at what exit.

We don't know exactly *how* the officials agreed to gauge 'friendly' among America's cities, but there are many other community categories we'd like to see some stats on:

- Top Ten Cities That Brag About Their Expansive Bike Paths
- Top Ten Cities That Have Leash Laws But Totally Ignore Them
- Top Ten Cities With A Street Named After A Deceased Local Politician
- Top Two Cities With A Street Named After An Unindicted Local Politician
- Top Ten Cities That Claim To Have The World's Widest Main Street
- Top Ten Cities With A Mayor Nicknamed "Cappy" or "Pud"
- Top Ten Cities That Claim To Have The World's Widest Mayor
- Top Ten Cities With Some Kind Of Festival That Celebrates A Salad Vegetable
- Top Ten Cities With Zoning Ordinances That Must've Been Designed By A Caffeine-Crazed Ferret
- Top Ten Cities That Have A Community College Offering A Degree In NASCAR Trivia
- Top Ten Cities Where A Local Politician Was Caught Having An Affair With A Ferret
- Top Ten Cities Having More Veterinarians Than Dentists
- Top Ten Cities With The Most Streets Whose Names Change Every Six Blocks Or So
- Top Ten Cities That Aren't Newark

So let's look a little closer at this year's most friendly (and most grumpy) cities.

2013's Top Ten Friendliest Cities in America

10. Branson, Missouri

Kicking off the list at #10 is Branson, Missouri, which I didn't even realize was an actual city...I thought it was a ride. So, if you think about it, feigning friendly in Branson isn't really a civic highlight; it's more of an HR requirement. It's just part of the job, like dancing in a cowboy-themed revue, or serving food in a place that requires you to wear a paper hat.

9. Sonoma, California

Sonoma: sounds like a sleeping pill. Nevertheless, the city's marketers bill Sonoma as "the down-to-earth alternative to Napa" -- in other words, "Hey! We got wine over here, too." Also on the city's website, they boast "We are pleased to have five wonderful Sister City Relationships" ... and then ... they list ... six cities.

Wine'll do that to ya.

8. Telluride, Colorado

The first thing we noticed on the city's website was the upcoming meeting of the Medical Marijuana Licensing Authority. And of course you know what *that* means: they have Twinkies in Telluride.

Twinkies & pot. An infallible formula for friendly.

7 & 6. Natchez and Jackson, Mississippi

We're sure that these cities are as friendly as the judges claim. Apparently, though, these two legendary hospitality centers house so many "Elvis Slept Here" plaques that it makes you wonder if "the King" was a narcoleptic. Or running for Congress.

5. Austin, Texas

Claiming the Friendly Cities' halfway spot is Austin, the capital of Texas, the Live Music Capital of the World, and, as if *that* weren't enough, host to the Ann Richards Congress Avenue Bridge Bats, North America's largest urban bat colony. (and that's *before* you count the capital politicians).

According to the city's website, visitors and hyper-friendly locals alike can, of an evening, gather at the bridge and watch as over 1.5 million nocturnal mammals dressed as former Texas Governor Ann Richards dart an escape into the twilight sky, as if they were Hillary Clinton being chased by a subpoena.

As one visitor sees things, Austin has a "young, healthy vibe." As another puts it, "Austin is weird."

4. Asheville, North Carolina

Let's cut to the chase. Acoustic music, microbreweries, moonshine, and pot. Phhh. No wonder they're friendly. Nobody's awake long enough to get grouchy.

3. Savannah, Georgia

Savannah is a fabulous city, nicely nestled along the Atlantic Ocean, with so much going for it that its citizens might justifiably be convivial simply because they get to live there. Unfortunately, President Obama recently told Jay Leno that Savannah is on the Gulf Coast. So now the city will have to move to the Gulf, else the IRS will audit everybody's lungs.

2. Galena, Illinois

Apparently, the marketing staff paid to promote this warmhearted western Illinois city didn't get the memo. They're still describing Galena as "quaint," which is the second-most overused phrase in American marketing, right behind "free gift."

We note that the city's website manages to brag about both Mississippi River vistas *and* top-shelf snow-skiing.

We think they're lying.

1. Charleston, South Carolina

Ah, Charleston. Rich history, graceful mansions, and Southern charm. Beaches, dining, and shopping. Gardens, ghosts, and the weirdest-smelling mud in this galaxy. And all of it wrapped in a humidity so thick it rivals canned paint.

Not for the first time, Charleston has yet again been voted America's friendliest city. It's been called the most polite city anywhere. This is true. According to one visitor, Charlestonians are "insanely" nice.

This is also true.

~-~-~-~-~-~

But let's not forget the other list!

Top Ten American Cities That Act Like There's An "Asinine Jerk" Nobel Prize

This won't take long. First of all, four of the Bottom Ten cities are in California, and five of the remaining six are in the Northeast. (oddly enough, none of them are infested with bridge bats dressed like Texas Governors)

10. Sacramento, California

When trying to describe the capital of the Golden State, the best one visitor could do was "a bit dingy."

It gets worse.

One promotional website warns us not to miss Sacramento's Fourth Annual Banana Festival, because ... ready? ... because it's "a-peeling."

There ought to be a law.

It gets worse. There's a five dollar admission fee to get into the Banana Festival. Now, *that's* bold. But we're not done yet. During the Banana Festival, some lucky lady will be crowned Miss Banana.

(Author's note: I would pay ten thousand dollars to hear comedian Lewis Black deliver that last sentence.)

According to the website, Miss Banana contestants must be at least 24 years old, and must be willing to accept - and I quote - "the duties of the crown, should she when."

Seriously. "Should she when."

It gets worse. There's a mandatory Miss Banana entry form that includes this burning question: "How do you intend to use your title as Miss Banana?"

That's just sad.

9 and so on. California, again

Peppering the rest of the poll are California's other unwelcome mats: Oakland, LA, and Anaheim (unfriendlies 2, 6, and 9, respectively).

Anaheim? Isn't that Disneyland? What, did somebody mug Mickey?

#8

We had hoped to offer you some insights about Wilmington, Delaware, Unfriendly City #8, but none of us has ever heard of it, and nobody could find it.

#5

Somehow Atlantic City made the cut, though we're not sure how. After all, the place is basically just one great big night club. Maybe Atlantic City should talk to Branson.

#4

Detroit made the American's Grumpiest list, but that's not really fair, since Detroit hasn't been part of America since, like, RoboCob.

#1

Newark, New Jersey.

Wonder what they did? Maybe they're just bitter, after going to all the trouble of building a whole city and everything, and then spending the rest of their lives being dismissively referred to as "the other airport."

~-~-~-~-~-~

By the way, we did check beyond our borders. There's also a "Top Ten Unfriendly Cities on Earth" poll. And the least friendly city on the whole planet?

It's still Newark. In fact, #2 on the list is Islamabad, Pakistan.

Digest *that* for a minute. Islamabad is runner up. *That's* how snarly Newark is.

~-~-~-~-~-~

But let's end on a happy note. The friendliest city in the entire world? Florianopolis, Brazil.

Among many other qualities, according to the internet, Florianopolis has an "excellent" airport. Right away we grew suspicious, as we tend to do when anybody wraps the word *excellent* in quotes. In our experience, when somebody says something is "excellent," it usually "sucks."

But that's just our "opinion."

Nothing To See Here, Folks

Don't like the news? Make up your own. They do.

<>~<>~~~~~~~~~~<>~<>~~~~~~~~~~<>~<>

This week, I didn't get to watch much television. Mostly because of the bleeding.

Remember my recent home disaster? The flood? Yeah, well, I spent most of this last week dealing with "insurance mitigation" - an activity which, for someone like me, mostly me involves banging into things because those things aren't where they used to be, pre-flood. You know what I mean -- pieces of my home that have been temporarily relocated for the "repair" stage: doors, kitchen appliances, rusted baseboard nails.

So it was late in the week before I could rejoin the world. But when I *did* get a minute to catch up on the news, it almost made me long for the flooding. Good caligulan grief -- grown men screaming at helpless children; news makers flipping the finger at news reporters; and samples of sexual dysfunction so bizarre, it made Richard III look like Richie Cunningham.

And that was just the Anthony Weiner headlines.

So, while I try to find where the flood cleanup team hid my Band-Aids, let's play a game we sometimes play round here. Here are some recent headlines...or not. Your job is to pick out the real ones. How hard could it be, right?

Right.

~-~-~-~-~-~

Anthony 'Carlos Danger' Weiner, ex-Congress, ex-Mayoral candidate, and ex-sane person, made the news when he:

a) yelled at a kid in a playground swing
b) yelled at a ragged homeless kitten that was blind and hadn't eaten in several days
c) inexplicably kept his mouth shut for ten minutes

Faced with financial default, looming budget deadlines, and a potential government shutdown, Congress decided to:

a) convene at noon
b) have the Senate re-carpeted
c) watch C-SPAN to see how it all worked out

In yet another 'zero tolerance' fiasco, a school principal noticed that a young student had a gun-shaped trinket on her charm bracelet. That's right: a quarter-inch, molded plastic charm. -- and for that 'violation,' the principal threatened to discipline the young girl. As a result:

a) the youngster was suspended
b) the child removed the offending trinket and stayed in detention after class

c) the kid shot him with the charm

The UN made news when:

a) Iran's visiting leader promised that his country's only purpose in developing nuclear energy is to power a exurban Baghdad dog fence, and then he backed up his oath with a pinky swear
b) that dagger-happy tribe of omnivores from Mel Gibson's movie *Apocalypto* was elected to lead the Human Rights Council
c) some diplomat actually parked legally

Sean Penn and Madonna made news when they:

a) decided to get back together again...again
b) made a suicide pact to vote Republican
c) didn't curse

Secretary of State John Kerry made news when he:

a) signed a controversial United Nations gun control treaty
b) erroneously blamed a terrorist attack on some Somali group named "Shish Kebob"
c) wore pants

An earthquake trembled Pakistan, and the associated seismic activity:

a) caused a new island to pop out of the ocean
b) caused Osama bin Laden to pop out of the ocean
c) sounded a lot like filmmaker Michael Moore at a taco buffet

Apple's new iPhone made news when:

a) first-week unit sales topped five million
b) first-week tech support calls topped ten million
c) Andrew Weiner sent a lewd photo to Siri, the voice assistant

Barack Obama, that legendary international negotiator, had a tough week. After being ignored by Syria's Assad, played by Russia's Putin, and snubbed by North Korea's Dennis Rodman, America's Waffler-in-Chief was totally dissed by Iran's Rouhani, who refused to take a meeting at the UN. However, the Script-Reader of the Free World took control of the situation when he:

a) sent Iran a smiley-face emoticon
b) decided, due to the breeze, to go with a six-iron
c) had another student hand Rouhani a folded-up note saying "Do u like me? Cirkel yes OR No"

The Pope made news when he:

a) lightened up on transgendered Millennials and atheists
b) announced the discovery of previously unknown Puccini opera named *Annie Domino*
c) fast-tracked the canonization of Barack Obama

The top-grossing movie for the first Autumn weekend was:

a) some movie featuring graphic violence among hapless strangers
b) some movie featuring graphic violence among transgendered Millennials
c) Iron Man XXIV: Pepper's Post-Partum Angst

When Iran's leader returned home from the UN, a protester threw a shoe at him. (Apparently, in the Muslim world, throwing a shoe at somebody is a nearly unforgivable insult, especially if the shoe is still attached to a suicide bomber.) After the shoe-lobbing incident, the Iranian protester:

a) was hailed as a counter-culture hero
b) had a soccer stadium named after him
c) had a soccer stadium built out of him

Two escaped felons made the news when they:

a) called 911 because they were lost
b) managed to *not* star in a Joel & Ethan Coen caper flick
c) were re-elected to Congress

Senator Ted Cruz made news on the Senate floor when he:

a) took the podium and spoke for twenty-one straight hours
b) acted out Adam Smith's *The Wealth of Nations* using three Muppets and a slide whistle
c) ate a live ferret

The Senate itself made news when:

a) nobody whatsoever showed up for the aforementioned twenty-one straight hours
b) they passed a non-binding resolution subsidizing Blue State ferrets
c) an entire week went by without a single federal indictment

When the Senator was asked why he staged the twenty-one-hour filibuster, the Senator:

a) said he was duty-bound to represent his constituency
b) claimed he'd planned to go even longer, but his aides forgot the other Dr. Seuss books

c) announced his corporate sponsor, Catheters-R-Us

According to a recent survey, 75% of guys:

a) would rather have a new iPhone than a girlfriend
b) think 'cloture' is some kind of hygiene product
c) will never get the joke in option b)

OJ Simpson made news when he:

a) stole a dozen cookies from a prison kitchen
b) killed the cookies
c) released a new book, "I Didn't Kill the Cookies, But If Had, Here's How I Would've Done It"

NASA's planetary rover, Curiosity, made news when it:

a) discovered water on Mars
b) discovered bottled water on Mars
c) killed a cat

~-~-~-~-~-~

To be sure, there were other bizarre, comment-worthy news stories this week...like the discomforting rumor about a woman that Bill Clinton couldn't seduce because Hillary got there first.

But I need to run. I'm bleeding again.

When I was getting out of the shower, I banged into a kitchen cabinet.

The Angst of Leisure

America. Putting the 'ax' in relax.

<>~<>~~~~~~~~~~<>~<>~~~~~~~~~~<>~<>

Now that the Winter Olympics have wrapped up, lots of Americans find themselves casting about, looking for something over which they can get overly emotional, for thirty minutes.

Minus commercials.

The "Honey? Have you seen my anxiety?" syndrome is a uniquely American neurosis. European nations, after an Olympics, just dive right back into their same-old, day-to-day, pre-Olympiad frustrations:

- putting up with American tourists who think the cure for not knowing the local language is to speak English loudly
- trying to remember what country you're driving in so you can curse appropriately

- pretending that, if we all just stay calm and don't encourage them, Greece will go away

Staying busy is easy for the Russians, too. Why, they had barely finished keeping the city of Sochi free from terrorists, wild dogs, and potentially gay Wheaties boxes, when some Ukrainian upstarts decided they wanted some of that 'freedom' nonsense everybody keeps going on about. So the Russian military just pivoted right, regrouped, and began a rousing game of "Boot on Neck."

(Barack Obama leaped into action. He had some staffer send a strongly-worded tweet to Vladimir Putin (@PapaBear), a no-nonsense missive containing a bold, take-no-prisoners number of frowny faces. According to inside sources, Putin's reply was an absolute masterwork of descriptive clarity; however, for Obama to accomplish the physical activity Putin suggested, he'd have to be *awfully* supple.)

So, for most of the world, the Olympics was a *break*...a *rest.* And the next Monday? Back to it. Heigh-ho, Heigh-ho. But Americans are another story. Americans are dying for something to worry about.

We're hungry to worry. We scour the media, online and off, looking to fling ourselves at guilt-soaked crusades like "Preserve Arbert Sprood's Homestead" and "Save Northeastern Louisiana's Last Indigenous Mottled Grey-Crested Migratory Ex-Methodist."

We've got it so good, we feel bad.

In fact, we don't even realize what we have. Americans have ... ready? ... Americans have *spare time.* Sure, you probably take spare time for granted, like going to a grocery with 250 types of former cheese, or buying a new gender. But for most cultures on Earth, an afternoon with no responsibilities would be like one of those nerve-wracking moments in *The Matrix* when you see the same cat walk by twice - some glitch that you just know means something seriously unpleasant is about to go down.

We're the most insecure successes in history. Okay, Napoleon. Napoleon was worse. And Yul Brynner in *The King and I.* But we're pretty needy. We like to be liked.

And that's where facebook steps in. When it comes to playing "Mirror, mirror, who's the fairest?", nothing can touch facebook. Facebook feeds the need to be liked. In fact, "liking" somebody is the number one action a person can take on facebook, except for typing LOL.

Facebook Insider Tip: When a person thinks something is really *really* funny, they may type LOLOL. Technically, this would translate as Laughing Out Loud Out Loud -- so you get some idea who you're dealing with here.

Another common self-flagellation technique on facebook is to post something, then count how many people like or share or comment about it. You've seen these desperation bombs, all of them, some variation of "When I find out how many people read my posts, I'll know if my life has value."

Hey, you can't argue with math.

This past week, I received such a post. It was begging to be lampooned, and I was up to the challenge. I copied it into a text editor, reworked it ruthlessly, and posted it myself.

I made the spoof as obviously satirical as I could stand ... or so I thought (more on that later). But I'll let you decide - here's my post:

~-~-~-~-~-~-~-~-~-~-~

A dear friend sent this to me and I thought to send it to you as well, my dear, dear facebook friends.

I am very selective when it comes to befriending friends and family; that's why I have several thousand, six of whom I've actually met. (Several thousand *friends*, not *family*. I've got *way* less family. As far as I know. Although I did date a Catholic girl once.)

This is a facebook test. I'm only doing this once, so here's your chance. I'm going to be watching to see who cares about friendship, just like me. I. Just like I. Do. Just like I do. Me do.

We'll see who takes the time to read this to the end. I already know who will and who won't. (of *course* I don't already know, but everybody says that)

If nobody reads my stuff, this will be a short experiment, after which I will kill myself, mix me up with old shrimp, and stuff the whole glop in your living room curtain rods.

So if you read this, and if you truly care about our friendship as much as I care about you, please copy this to *your* wall -- don't *share* it, for Pete's sake, *COPY IT!* -- then pick 350 of your closest friends and buy all of them 4 or 5 of my books.

Then leave one word on how we met. (shut up, Catholic girl)

Only one word. Then I'll leave a word. Then you leave a word, then I'll leave a word, and so on, until one of us snaps and beats the other one unconscious.

Have an LOL day!

~-~-~-~-~-~-~-~-~-~-~

And, lo and behold, dozens of people actually replied with "one word on how we met" ... though several were apparently stumped by the "one" part of "one word."

Please tell me you picked up some of the subtle clues in the post above that *shrieked* 'SATIRE.'

Really? Not even the part where I threatened to Ginsu myself into shrimp salad?

No?

Not even the part where I had a date?

Snooki Debriefs the Pentagon

What if you threw a war and nobody came?

<>~<>~~~~~~~~~~<>~<>~~~~~~~~~~<>~<>

Remember the good old days of American politics? The days when larger-than-life statesmen would assemble in all-night debates over matters of global import, delivering stentorian speeches in the halls of Congress, making point after point after relentless, logical point, until they finally won the day by beating each other half to death with canes?

And that's where it gets weird. That's how far we haven't come. Compared to what passes for political discourse today, I miss the canes.

These days in DC, sanity was spotted wearing stilettos in the men's room, and coherent debate is in rehab. Policy is something you buy from Allstate. A politician can be pushing the most insane policy imaginable ... like, say, going to war with Syria - but only for a few minutes, we promise! ... all the pol has to do is sell it to the right idols.

To shove out a flawed agenda in today's White House, you don't need intelligence. You need endorsements.

What matters is messaging. Public Relations. Group emotion. Me too, you betcha, amen, ditto, durn tooty. What matters is what famous people think, because everybody wants to be famous people.

And the endorsements that close the deal are the ones from studied, globally-minded thinkers in deeply cerebral, highly relevant careers: mid-afternoon talk show hosts, money-hating money-grabbing movie stars, transgendered jocks.

So we cobbled together our own little one-question survey: should America take immediate military action in Syria, as long as it doesn't happen during *American Idol*? And here's where everybody stands.

Everybody that counts, that is.

~-~-~-~-~-~

Harry Reid, Senate Leader and Nevada's premier pork shoveler, fully supports the action...allegedly...but the odd little man mumbles so badly that nobody's actually understood anything *he's* said since about 1956.

The Amazing Kreskin predicted that the White House would withdraw its war plans after the President's wife told him that Syria was our 57th State. The mentalist then offered to divine what Congress was thinking, but the overwhelming irony of that statement collapsed the auditorium floor.

Nancy Pelosi, ex-House Speaker and Botox Overdose poster child, surprised no one as she stood behind the President and said she stood behind the President. But that's the kind of deep geopolitical wisdom the world has come to expect from a woman with the grin of a punch clown and the intelligence of an asparagus fern. (We're still trying to figure out why she walks like she does. She looks like someone whose feet were surgically removed, but the hospital forgot to tell her.)

Former *24* uber-agent Jack Bauer wants to fight, but he wants to fight with a CTU team that we know for a fact was killed last season.

A collective "No" was logged by several Bushes, including George 'Dubya' Bush, George 'Aitch Dubya' Bush, Barbara Bush, Jeb Bush, Kate Bush, and that annoying dog that shills for Bush's Baked Beans.

The IRS said they were in favor of military action. The NSA snickered and told the IRS they already knew that. But according to the DOJ, that's not what the IRS told its wife last night at dinner in that CIA tent by the DHS lake. Fortunately, the FBI confirmed the IRS's alibi, and so the NSA whistleblowers were shot down by heavily-armed sharpshooters from the National Weather Service. The IRS then proceeded with its plan to spend 27 million dollars on a training video featuring Gilligan and the Skipper line-dancing with Uhura and Spock on the bridge of the *USS Enterprise.*

Obviously, John Kerry, the Secretariat of State, is for whatever the President tells him he's for. Later this week, Kerry's scheduled to speak to French people in France (you have to lay things out very clearly for Mr. Kerry). Handlers say Kerry will cover topics ranging from what fork to use when you're having dinner with an ophthalmologist-cum-mass murderer, to making little *I HEART OBAMA* shapes out of truffle bibs. Afterwards, Kerry is hosting a sold-out seminar on how to fake injuries and throw your medals over a fence.

Yahoo's sparkling new CEO, Marissa Mayer, is on record as 'against' lots of different nasty things, including war and men who treat her like an object. (When we reached Mme. Mayer, she was lying upside-down on a Scandinavian chaise as part of a sultry photo shoot for *Vogue*.)

Crusty old actor/activist Ed Asner appears to be against military action. We think. With that face, it's hard to tell. Either he's surly about Syria, or he just bit into a bad oyster.

Senator Dianne Feinstein is absolutely slavering to give a bunch of weapons to Syrian citizens - maybe the goose-stepping buttinski's devious little plan is to give Syrians the guns she's trying to take away from Americans.

Dennis Rodman, famous basketball player and nose magnet, had no comment on the Syrian situation; he's too busy playing Far East diplomat again. Tackling a delicate negotiation to secure the release of an incarcerated missionary, Rodman asked North Korea's leader, Kim Erica Jong, to "do him a solid." Little Kim nodded confusedly, slugged another 18-ounce Scotch, and mailed Rodman a small cube.

Senator John McCain is afraid we'll shoot at too many things, and he's afraid we won't shoot at enough things. Personally, we think maybe John needs to go lie down for a while.

Geraldo Rivera said he's firmly in support of military action against Syria, or Aruba, or anyone else for that matter. Then, having completed an entire sentence without talking about himself, he quickly queued up another film clip of himself, breathlessly duck-running across some generic airstrip somewhere, wearing a military-issue helmet and what appears to be several people's facial hair.

Al Gore thought the "war" question was moot, and suggested everybody use that "peace" thing he'd invented.

Poxltektocotl, a 1400-year-old Aztec pundit and second-tier panther deity, wisely took no sides in the Syrian conflict, but recommends that if the President *does* plan on bumping ugly, he better look slippy about it, 'cause...you know...doom, rock calendar, end-of-all-things. Tick tock. Apocalypso. I'm just sayin'.

When approached, France just kept yelling "Vive! Vive! Vive!" as if lobbing misspelled paper towels at the enemy was a winning tactical plan. But then, it *is* France.

A hasty anti-war coalition was ginned up between Rand Paul, Ron Paul, Mrs. Paul, RuPaul, John Paul II, Paul McCartney, Paul Bunyan, and both Paul Simons. In addition to denouncing the Syrian military action, Ron Paul demanded that America withdraw all its troops from RuPaul.

The *Duck Dynasty* crew, fed up with all these news interruptions during college football season, seemed ready to resolve matters, - and quickly - by sending in Phil Robertson to "tear their tail up." As Uncle Si put it, "Look. Phil'll put a end to all this putterin' and nonsense, Jack. Hey." When asked by the international press why the Robertsons were sending just one man with one gun, Phil replied, "Son, there ain't but one war."

Jane Fonda flew in her non-solar-powered, huge-carbon-footprint private jet to a rally in Tehran to show her support for the Religion of Peace, but she removed her hat in public and somebody cut off her head.

Somehow, during all the pre-war planning, the hardly Reverend Al Sharpton found an unguarded microphone and started ranting like Renfield on a meth binge, until a nearby airport called in to complain about the glare from his hair oil.

And Mitt Romney, for his part, mostly just kept quiet and shook his head. But not his hair.

Plane Talk

If men were meant to fly, we'd have been born with peanuts.

<>~<>~~~~~~~~~~<>~<>~~~~~~~~~~<>~<>

I don't like airports. Mostly because being in airports leads to being in airplanes. And *being* in airplanes can lead to *flying* in airplanes, eventually, though these days, you never know.

These days, if you must travel, it makes more sense to just drive to your destination, unless you're going to some foreign country, like Iran, or Detroit. For me, flying holds *zero* allure, what with all the downsides: the prices; the pre-flight security; the takeoff and landing delays; the weather delays; the lost baggage delays; the risk of getting a window seat next to Tom DeLay.

Hassles aside - and they are legion - I don't care for any activity where the primary instruction is "stay calm."

But don't take *my* word for it. Here...I'll let the airport speak for itself:

~-~-~-~-~-~

In the Airport

[*Disembodied Female Voice*]

Welcome to the Midtown International Airport, and to another slog through the grueling and dehumanizing gauntlet that is airline travel. Congratulations on having deciphered the various parking options, and for having avoided crippling injury or violent death in the curb-side pickup/drop-off lanes - an area we affectionately refer to as "The Ego Coliseum."

You are now in the Main Ticketing Concourse, which may contain the nastiest piece of no-culture carpet in the solar system. For your convenience, we have removed all references to the *real* world outside, including windows, clocks, and realistically priced food. On a personal note, the baggage handlers at Midtown International would like to thank you for showing up with more luggage than Ike used to invade Europe.

At this time, please spend a few irritating hours trying to find the check-in desk for your chosen airline, from whom you optimistically ordered tickets online, and which we forgot to mention is now operating under another name, at the far end of the Midtown International concourse complex, which is located in Cleveland.

Until then, we hope you'll enjoy lugging your checked and carry-on tonnage back and forth, back and forth, back and forth, through our highly configurable, bank-teller-style, customer queue walking trails, a switchback system that converts a direct four-step walk into a winding, eleven-mile trek, using a design based on a 90-year-old Parisian cheese-maker's small intestine.

And speaking of impacted bowels, don't forget to visit our convenient bar and dining area, the Tarmac 'N' Cheese, where you can experience the culinary confusion of paying five bucks for a dry cookie that tastes like it might have been a *Sesame Street* stage prop, or sip a cocktail while pondering the marketing mindset that led to shamelessly charging $17.50 for Eve's original apple and a ptomaine-teased tuna fish sandwich.

Before your flight issues its "boarding now" announcement, which could be, oh, just any day now, be sure to visit our gift shop, the Shuttle Crock, filled floor-to-ceiling with chintzy local mementos, inedible snacks, and bulky, hardback copies of books by every author you can imagine, as long as you imagine Dan Brown and Danielle Steele.

And folks, please remember, in case you've been in a coma for the last twenty years and didn't get the memo: this is a non-smoking facility, just like every other structure in America that has a roof, including your own car.

~-~-~-~-~-~

In the Airplane

[*Disembodied Male Voice*]

Ladies and gentlemen, your attention, please. This is the Captain. We've received clearance from the tower to begin cautiously hoping for a conceivably eventual takeoff, which my co-pilot and I estimate should put us in the #1 position on the runway sometime between, say, 4:46pm and the next major continental shift.

At this time I'll ask everyone to return to their assigned seats, buckle up, and try to relax, even though your seats are so ancient they still have ashtrays in the armrests, and despite the fact that those seats, we're pretty sure, are firmly bolted to a lowest-bid plane that we've been using since women wore velour gauchos.

Now, please direct your attention to the front of the cabin for the Obligatory Safety Lecture. And, again, thank you for flying Deep Budget Cuts Airlines.

~-~-~-~-~-~

[*Steward-person of the female persuasion with savagely white dental work*]

Hi! My name's Binkie, and on behalf of Deep Budget Cuts Airlines, may I say 'thank you' for flying with us today, assuming all things go well. We're grateful to you for choosing our airline, and for submitting to a full-body cavity search by a uniformed, snotty, staggeringly undertrained, 350-pound civil servant!

In just a brief moment, we'll ask that you please direct your attention to the front of the cabin, where, as part of the Obligatory Safety Lecture, we will present a short film on our

Deep Budget Cuts custom 16-mm movie screen with that slight tilt and the duct-taped patches.

But first things first! Please take a moment to find the plane's exits, which I'm more-or-less pointing to now with these vague semaphore-like arm gestures. It's important that you plan, in advance, how to reach the exit nearest you in the unlikely event of a life-ending tragedy while flying at 300 miles per hour, some 30,000 feet above a bunch of really hard landscape, in a 42-year-old metal tube that's theoretically being maintained by a bitter, underpaid mechanics union.

And remember! While you're blindly groping for the nearest exit in hellish, smoke-filled darkness as you plummet inexorably into gravity's grip, please remain calm.

Under your seat is a 1960s-era flotation device that is utterly useless, given our departure and destination points. I mean, the chances of this flight landing in an ocean are about as likely as Michelle Obama offering to 'go dutch' on a hotel bill.

And now let's turn to the topic of staying calm during sudden cabin decompression, which is a common side-effect of colliding with a rogue asteroid duri...

[*Eighty-seven minutes later*]

...and in the unlikely event that anyone *should* discharge a weapon, regardless of their Constitutionally-guaranteed religious orientation, please use the provided stationery to write to your Congressperson about gun ownership, while remaining calm.

Finally, should we experience a water event (don't even ask), please figure out how to put on part of your seat, and how to fend off sharks with that lame in-flight meal knife, while remaining calm.

Thank you for your attention, and please enjoy this spot-welded foil bag that contains two peanuts.

~-~-~-~-~-~

Nope. Not for me. I'm driving to the business meeting in Cleveland. See you at the hotel.

I'll be the one that's on time.

With all those peanuts.

A Form and a Fee

How to become an American ... the hard way

<>~<>~~~~~~~~~~<>~<>~~~~~~~~~~<>~<>

Late last week, one of the best people I know became an American citizen. So, once he was on *our* team, I did the patriotic thing: I turned him in to the NSA.

It was the first time I'd ever attended a citizenship swearing-in ceremony, if you don't count one extremely social après-football event in college that I'm still advised not to discuss. (I dimly remember that uniforms were involved then, too ... though not much civics.)

Since I'd never been to one, I had no idea what to expect. I wasn't even sure what one wears as the guest of a fledgling citizen. My new American friend was wearing a tie for his big day, but if you know me at all, you know *that* wasn't happening. As a rule, if you see me sporting a tie, you can be sure that one of three things is happening:

1) I'm up for parole

2) I'm in an ornate room filled with sniffling people, lots of flowers, and an expensive oblong box
3) I'm in the box

I compromised. And me and my matching socks drove into town, soon pulling in to the offices of the U.S. Citizenship and Immigration Services.

As it turns out, I'd seen the USCIS building before - it was right across the street from the Post Office (as an independent author, I'm constantly running by the Post Office to not pick up royalty checks). The parking lot was packed - apparently, there were still lots of potential citizens who hadn't gotten the memo about the "discount" citizenship plan: sneaking into the country.

Assuming you've managed to park, the first thing you see inside the USCIS building is an airport. Or you would think. Cold counters, id checks. Gray trays and black bowls to hold your keys, your wallet, your belt, your remote detonators. Conveyor belt X-ray machines and walk-through metal detectors. Armed, uniformed guards with unblinking lizard eyes and a sense of humor like Hitler in a bunker. The only thing missing were the infamous TSA pat-downs, but here in the South, that could be misconstrued as a marriage proposal.

Taped to the counter was a "don't even think about it" list of things you're not supposed to bring to a swearing-in; you know, box cutters, socks that explode, bomb-fused Fruit-of-the-Looms, stuff like that. Topping the list: knives with blades less than two-and-a-half inches. I guess it's okay to prance around USCIS with a cavalry sword, or a scimitar, or a large pointy stick. (In fact, Joe Biden does it all the time. In a loincloth. And stiletto heels.)

After retrieving our wallets and detonators, we were ushered into an overfilled, pending-citizen-packed room, where we were greeted by two USCIS employees whose names, I think, were "Officer Lady" and "The Suit." The nearly-Americans were seated in a center clutch of chairs, and the families and guests filled the chairs, walls, and the rest of the room.

At the front of the room was a nondescript lectern, a really bored table, and two American flags. Mounted to the wall between the flags were two large-screen TVs, both made by Sharp, and both inexplicably displaying "Samsung" in giant letters on the screen. Adorning a side wall were government-issue framed photos of occasionally-president Barack Obama, ex-cabineteer Janet Napolitano, and some solemn balding guy I didn't recognize...maybe he's the federal drone in charge of teaching federal security guards how to not blink for eight straight hours. On the near wall were the school cafeteria-style doors through which we'd all entered, and on the far wall, a single emergency exit door. Glued to the door was a bright red warning: THIS DOOR IS ALARMED.

I thought that was a very honest attitude for the door to have. After all, the first step toward recovery is admitting you have a problem.

Given the lack of seating, I stood there along the far wall, next to the edgy exit, until Officer Lady "suggested" I not block that door. I, of course, immediately obeyed, since I am an unquestioning admirer of authority figures, and since she was armed.

After a short wait, the ceremony officially began. Officer Lady welcomed everyone and then reached for ... well, nothing. Apparently, some USCIS underling had forgotten to set out some of Officer Lady's props on the lectern. (These "where's my thingie" miscues happened about five times during the course of the forty-five-minute event. Normally, this is a level of incompetence reserved for the IRS.)

Officer Lady made it through the prelims, and then Mr. Suit took the podium. But before he could really get rolling, he was interrupted by somebody's family member who wanted to know if Mr. Suit was from the "Stone Hill" area, 'cause the interrupter knows lots of people by that name, up there in the Stone Hill area. Fortunately, we got back on track after one of the other guests stabbed the disrupter with a scimitar.

Mr. Suit then announced that one of the traditions in this USCIS branch was a little something they liked to call the "Country Call-Off." Mr. Suit would read off the home country of each new American, and that citizen-to-be would stand up and be recognized.

Sadly, though, somebody had forgotten to pre-load the podium with the list of countries.

Brave Mr. Suit pushed on. He had everyone watch a "short presentation" titled "Faces of America," which seemed mostly to be a 100-year collage of arguments for good dental care. Then he had everyone watch a "short presentation" by Barack

Obama, which went well until the President misread his in-screen teleprompter cues and actually said, out loud, "Pause. Bite lip." Finally, Mr. Suit had everyone watch a "short presentation" of Lee Greenwood singing what is, apparently, the only song Lee Greenwood knows.

Finally, with a majestic federal underling flourish, Mr. Suit held high the stack of official US citizenship certificates, causing the entire crowd to almost stop texting. But before distributing the docs, Mr. Suit had to ferry the citizens-on-deck through a litany of "a form and a fee" disclaimers. To get a replacement certificate, there'd be a form and a fee. To register their children, there was a form and a fee. To apply for a passport, there'd be a form and a fee, and passport applications can be processed at any US Post Office.

Well, said Mr. Suit, any US Post Office except the one right across the street. *That* Post Office doesn't accept USCIS certificates as valid ID.

Welcome to America.

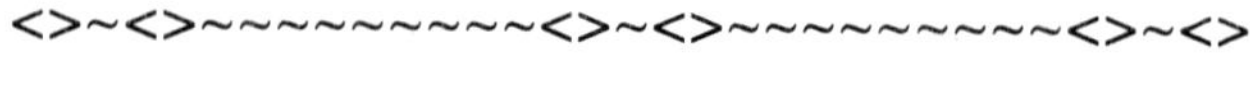

###

About the Author

Barry Parham is a recovering software freelancer and the author of humor columns, essays and short stories. He is a music fanatic and a 1981 honors graduate of the University of Georgia.

Writing awards and recognitions earned by Parham include taking First Place in the November 2009 Writer's Circle Competition, First Prize in the March 2012 writing contest at HumorPress.com, and a plug by the official website of the Erma Bombeck Writers' Workshop. Most recently, Parham's work has appeared in three national humor anthologies.

Author's website
http://www.barryparham.com

@ facebook
http://www.facebook.com/pmWriter

@ Twitter
http://twitter.com/barryparham

@ Google+
http://tinyurl.com/n6w5gq4